Little Buddha Book T

Karen & Tim

It is one of my fondest wishes that you are enjoying moving along with Claire & Sam and the others and finding joy here.

Love,
Tod

Little Buddha
Book Two

Rob H. Geyer

Little Buddha Book Two

Little Buddha Book Two

Copyright ©2018 Rob H. Geyer

All rights reserved.

ISBN-13: 978-1722963507

ISBN-10: 1722963506

Little Buddha Book Two

Little Buddha Book Two

Dedication

To my mother and father, Dorothy and Howard, for their unwavering love and support throughout my life. They are a blessing to me.

And

To my wife's and my children, Jenny and Tommy, who are two of the bright and shinning stars of our lives.

Little Buddha Book Two

From the Author

I have been listening to god's voice my whole life. I've found that it comes to me in many ways, some more mysterious than others, but all of them filled with love. This book is a continuation of Sam and Claire's story. I feel so touched that they keep sharing their words, feelings and love with me. I hope you enjoy hearing them speak to you through the words of this book. If you'd like to contact me, my e-mail address is:

littlebuddha483@ gmail.com.

Blessings to you,
Rob

Little Buddha Book Two

Table of Contents

homecoming 1
more room 14
the nature of water..32
"I am…" 51
String theory 68
sparks 88
seeds 109
change orders...133
Sign language...148
New beginnings 163
exercises for going deeper 183
homecoming 185
the nature of water...194
"i am…" 199
string theory 205
sparks 211
seeds 218
change orders..223
sign language 228
new beginnings..234
Little Buddha Book Two Notes 239

Little Buddha Book Two

homecoming

Little Buddha Book Two

I'd come earlier in the morning than usual, so I glanced over the top of their fence to see if Claire or Janine were up and around. What I saw was a beautifully decorated yard with banners and streamers everywhere. One of the banners read, 'welcome home sunshine' and another said, 'happy eleventh birthday Claire'. Somehow, I'd forgotten it was her birthday today, this most wonderful, special child. I was so excited to see her again. It had been several months and I had missed her and her mom very much.

It's funny how you miss seeing things when you're so focused on only one thing. I wanted so much to be with her and had completely missed noticing all of the hearts Claire and Janine and I had painted and hung up last summer. They were everywhere along their fence leading to the beach. I was tempted to count them, but I already knew there were three hundred and thirty-three, because Claire and I hung every one of them up ourselves. It truly was an awesome sight. I remember her telling me that the number was significant to her, but as was pretty common for her, she didn't tell me why. Instead, she asked me to think about it and she'd tell me when I came back the next summer. Well, here I was.

Little Buddha Book Two

Just then, Janine, Claire's mom, came out of their cottage and saw me.

"Hi Sam, welcome home."

She said it like I belonged there. It felt so good to me to be wanted. Over the years I had developed such love for her and for her daughter, my mentor, my friend, my very own little Buddha.

I opened the gate and we hugged each other. "It's so nice to see you Janine," I said, "how are you?"

"I'm divine," she said. The way she said it and the way her energy radiated outward to everyone in her life, I totally believed she was divine.

"Where's Claire," I asked, "I thought she'd be here."

"She'll be here this morning," Janine answered, "she's been visiting her father and grandfather out west for the past month". Her eyes met mine. They were so beautiful, almost the color of violet. I'd never seen anyone with that color eyes before, simply incredible. "She'll be so happy to see you," Janine said.

Little Buddha Book Two

I was wondering now about her father. We'd never spoken about him in all the time I'd known her. I wanted to ask, but it felt wrong somehow, so I just smiled and said, "I've missed her so much and can't wait to see her," then added, "I've missed you too." She smiled in return.

Just then we heard the sound of a car door closing in the front yard. I heard a voice I recognized so well.

"Hi, I'm home," Claire called out.

Janine and I both ran to their front door, then out into their yard.

Claire took her two bags from the driver, set them down and spread out her arms toward him. He leaned down to hug her and then lifted her in the air. His face was turned toward Janine and me and I could see his expression. It was a look of utter joy and peace and I could actually feel the energy radiating from both of them.

After the driver set her down, Claire took out some money from her pocket and handed it to him, along with what looked like a handwritten note, like the ones I used to pass around when

Little Buddha Book Two

I was a kid in school. He took the money and started to unfold the note. She placed her hand gently over his and said, "Why don't you read that later, Maheer, it's kind of personal."

He seemed very surprised but refolded it and stuck it back in his jacket.

"It was a pleasure to spend time with you," Claire said.

"Oh no, my precious one, the pleasure was mine." The driver bowed, got back in his taxi and drove off.

Janine and I rushed toward Claire and we both hugged her at the same time. What a delight! We stepped back, looked at each other and then at Claire. "Happy birthday," we chimed in unison, like we'd practiced it all day.

"It's so awesome to see you both," she said. "Mom, everyone said to say 'hi' to you and let you know they miss you and hope you'll come for a visit soon."

Janine nodded and I wondered who they were talking about. I'd ask later.

Little Buddha Book Two

Janine held out her arms with her palms facing toward Claire. Claire did the same and came closer so that their palms touched. Then they interlaced fingers and brought their foreheads together. I could see how much Claire had grown since I'd last seen her. She was almost as tall as her mom. For a moment they looked like twins, both so beautiful. I felt so fortunate to know them and to be able to spend time with them. It was then that something struck me as odd. I'd never seen them embrace like this before. I was about to comment when they both turned toward me and Janine said, "This is our reunion ceremony. We do it every time we've been away from each other for a while. It helps us to reconnect and rebalance."

Claire said, "Sam, I want to reconnect with you too. I've missed you a lot and am so happy to see you. She motioned for me to come over to their front steps. She climbed up one step so we'd be closer in height, then held out her palms toward me. I walked over, raised my arms up and interlaced my fingers with hers. I immediately felt an enormous energy rush. It seemed like my whole body was vibrating. It felt so amazing.

Claire leaned her head toward me with her eyes looking directly into mine. They were

Little Buddha Book Two

simply mesmerizing, so luminous and alive. I leaned forward until our foreheads touched. I was not prepared for the incredible jolt I received. It was positively electric, but instead of that horrible feeling you get from static electricity, it felt enlivening and wonderful. My body felt awake and refreshed. This kind of reunion almost made up for missing her.

We all went inside to their kitchen and Janine poured us some iced tea.

I couldn't wait to hear about Claire's trip, but I was too intrigued with the whole 'taxi driver note passing thing'.

Before I could ask, she turned and said, "He's a very special man and he's had a life filled with great loss. He's from the Middle East and he's lost his whole family and he fears he's lost a great part of himself. He believes he deserves his suffering and so I wrote him a note to tell him the truth."

"Which is what?" I asked.

Claire bowed her head a little, looked at the ground and then back up at me. "I told him that no one 'deserves' pain. That life can and does feel very unfair sometimes. That nothing can

Little Buddha Book Two

undo what has been done, but that others can and will come into his life. They will bring him love, if he will allow it. I told him that he has so much still to give and receive and that life renews itself if your heart is open. I told him that I love him and that I see his heart and there is room there. I asked him if he would let me in and let me love him. I gave him my phone number and told him he could call me any time he wished."

I was so moved by her words, her open, giving, loving heart. How could I be so fortunate that she was in my life. I silently gave thanks for her presence in the world. I gazed at her, so overcome, I was teary eyed.

She looked back at me, "I know Sam, I love you too," she said.

It seemed that everyone was hungry, so Janine set out all sorts of food for us to choose from. My diet had certainly changed since I'd spent so much time with them. I'd become more aware of what I put into my body and it made a huge difference in the way I felt.

We sat down and I couldn't wait any longer. "Claire where were you, what did you do there,

Little Buddha Book Two

did you learn new things, have you had any visions…come on, spill it."

She and Janine both laughed at me. Oh, so what I thought and laughed too.

"I know," I said, "I can't help it. I know I asked several questions. How about this, could you at least answer one? You can pick it."

Claire's forehead creased a tiny bit and she seemed a little pensive. "Okay Sam, I'll tell you about one of my conversations with Bright Sky, my grandfather.

"One day we went for a walk and came upon a forest of trees. We marveled at their beauty and their dancing leaves in the wind. The air around us was so fresh and the sun warmed our bodies. We sat among the trees for hours without moving. When we finally arose, Bright Sky said to me, "Well Nexahe, that was a good experience for heaven."

He turned and held out his hands to me. I gave my hands to him and he spoke these words. "Granddaughter, everything you experience here, the great spirit experiences and those in the great beyond also experience. You are their breathe, their eyes, their heart. What happens to you, happens to them."

Claire looked at me. "Do you understand this Sam?"

I suspect she knew my answer. "Not really."

"At the time, I did not either," she said.

This really surprised me. I thought she knew everything. I probably was being foolish, after all she was only eleven, but she'd always known the answers to all of my questions. I was intrigued by what Bright Sky had told her but wasn't sure what he'd meant. "Can you tell me more?" I asked.

Claire shifted in her seat as if she was somewhat uncomfortable. "Sam, I'm still receiving the lesson he shared with me, but I'll try."

"Grandfather started by telling me about the aspen grove. He asked me to gaze at the forest and tell him what I saw. I told him I saw an exquisite, abundant array of trees that felt alive and playful because their leaves fluttered constantly in the breeze."

Little Buddha Book Two

"How many trees do you see?", he asked.

The trees spread far and wide, "Perhaps a thousand, maybe more," I answered.

He smiled and shook his head.

"Are there more?", I asked.

"No," he said, "there is only one."

"But Grandfather," I said, "how can that be?"

"I understand your confusion, Nexie. It is because you are counting what you see on the surface with your eyes. If you could see below the ground you would see the truth. Every tree is connected to every other tree because they share the same roots underground. In this way, what happens to one, happens to them all. They 'appear' to be separate, but they are not, they are one essence. For the aspen, they share the air and water, the sun and the soil, the sky and all that live above and below the surface of mother earth. What one experiences, they all experience."

We were quiet for a moment then he said, "It works the same way with each of us. What we experience in our lives here on the surface of mother earth is also experienced by all essences in the great beyond, what you call heaven."

"Does that mean that they experience all of our pain and suffering?"

Bright Sky looked deeply into me and saw the hurt in my heart and answered, "Not in the way you might imagine, nor in the way you fear. They receive the energy being experienced, but they transform it with love." He smiled at me and I was immediately at peace.

"Imagine that you see a fierce rain storm coming toward us. The clouds are black and threatening and you hear the thunder roar. Imagine this represents the pain and suffering you sometimes feel and experience here. Now, shift your gaze to the other side of the sky. Imagine there is sunshine and a slight mist and there, arcing through the sky, is a magnificent rainbow. Imagine this represents the transformative power of love, which creates beauty out of any perception of suffering, pain or despair."

I sat and absorbed this for a while. I could see his word picture clearly. I was struggling with the idea of how the transformation happened. I

Little Buddha Book Two

asked, "Grandfather, you're saying that despite what we experience here on earth, the one essence in heaven receives what we feel, then transforms it with love?"

"Yes."

"Grandfather, that's so beautiful. Can we do that same thing here on earth? Can we transform our perception of pain and suffering through love?"

He was quiet for a long time and I was drawn in to his silence. I listened to his breathing and aligned mine with his. His contentment passed to me.

"Yes, granddaughter we can, if we choose it. If we shift enough of our perceptions, if it becomes our radiant intention and our constant choice, yes, we can. It is a form of practice. Each of us has the power to pour our love over any experience and shift the thunder into the rainbow."

"Thank you for opening my heart grandfather. Will you share more with me about this, about how to make this shift?"

"Yes, on another walk, dear one.

Little Buddha Book Two

more room

Little Buddha Book Two

The day started out with brilliant sunshine, but by the time I'd arrived at Claire's cottage the clouds had moved in. They thickened and turned a deep gray, completely blocking out the sun. I have to say it was really affecting my mood. I felt like something dark had taken over a part of me.

I had been thinking about the story Claire had told me a couple of years ago. The one where the young girl had awoken and started walking on a path that led to a large round building. I remember she went in the only door and found that the only thing in the room was a chair. I'm pretty sure the chair swiveled in a full circle so whoever sat there could spin completely around. The chair had a small toggle switch on the arm that moved in a full circle too. At the time she told me the story I imagined how awesome it would be to sit in the chair, because as soon as you thought of an event from your life, you would see the event visually on the wall of the building. It displayed all around you, as if it was happening all over again. The detail was so vivid and spectacular. I imagined how incredible it would be to "relive" beautiful events from my life and to "feel" and "see" every detail. And then, even more incredibly, I could experience the event from another people's perspective just be moving

Little Buddha Book Two

the toggle switch toward their image on the screen. Wow! It seemed to me that it would be fantastic to be able to shift from my consciousness to theirs and then to be able to see what changed in their life because of our connection. And not only how it affected them but the others their life touched. I remember thinking how magnificent it would be to feel the joy, but I also had a nagging feeling I couldn't shake. I wondered, what about all those times that my experiences were painful? And what about the times I was the cause? The times I created suffering, especially for the people I loved the most. Knowing there was this possibility, I wasn't so sure I wanted to do this kind of life review.

Well, I was here at the gate to her backyard. I peered into the yard. No one was around, but as part of her "family" I felt I could just go in, so I did. As I walked toward her back door I saw her standing in front of their large plate glass window. I felt like the sun had just come back out and my dark mood immediately lifted. I was home.

"Good morning sunshine," I said, as I opened the door and our eyes met.

Little Buddha Book Two

"I see you," she said. She placed one of her hands on my heart and took one of my hands and placed it on her heart. "You mean something to me," she intoned.

We stood there like that for maybe two minutes. It was pure heaven to me. To have someone in my life who I knew loved ME. Saw ME. Cared about ME. She was my connection to the divine.

"Sam," she said, "someday you will feel this way about everyone."

I wanted to believe her, but I couldn't at this point. There were too many cracks and fissures in my life, I hoped she was right, but I certainly couldn't say it was my truth right then.

"I hope so," I responded, "but so many things have occurred in my life, I'm just not sure how that could happen."

"That's okay Sam, we have all the time in the world."

She was smiling so radiantly that I believed anything was possible in her world.

Little Buddha Book Two

"I have a surprise for you," she said, as she led me into their living room. "Sit right here please and close your eyes. We're going to relax into some music and take a journey.

She pressed the button on her sound system and ethereal music filled the room. It was enchanting and I began to relax almost immediately.

"Where are we going on our journey?", I asked.

"Into your glorious past," she responded.

"Not all of my past in glorious you know," I stated, perhaps a bit more emphatically than I'd intended.

I could hear her breathing. It was slow and smooth and easy. I felt my breathing mirror hers. I always loved this. It was as if she was breathing for me. After a few minutes, I found my own rhythm and felt even more relaxed.

"Sam, I want to invite you to go into 'the room' with me. You know the one I mean, the one you were thinking about on your walk here this morning. See yourself enter the room. Walk around until you are comfortable then sit in the

Little Buddha Book Two

chair and notice where the toggle switch is. Keep breathing, slow and steady. Shift your attention to your feet as they rest on the floor. Feel inside of you that you are breathing for the earth. You are connected and aware of the grounding energy that supports you. Rest here."

I did as she asked. It was wonderful.

"Now feel the divine energy entering through the top of your head and moving downward through your whole body. Shift your attention to your heart, where the two energies become one. Let the energy grow. Feel your heart beat and know you are part of the divine."

I'd never experienced this before. We'd done lots of different meditations, but nothing like this. I felt so at peace.

"Sam," Claire whispered, "let's take a journey back through your life. I'm going to ask you to choose one event. I realize a part of you is afraid. That's okay, I'm with you, right here with you. I want you to know that every part of your life is glorious. There is nothing to be afraid of. I know you don't see this yet. Trust me. We'll do this together. Okay?"

Little Buddha Book Two

I admit it. My breathing changed as she spoke. I was afraid. There were events in my life I didn't want to relive. I had a great deal of reluctance inside of me. What if I got stuck inside one of my bad memories?

I wondered too, how could she claim that everything was 'glorious'? I was pretty sure it wasn't. But some part of me wanted to see, to know if there was a greater truth. Something that could make sense out of my painful experiences. And I did trust her. I trusted her with my whole life. So, I continued breathing and found a way to reclaim my peace. She must have noticed because I heard her say, "Thank you Sam for trusting me."

I drifted a bit with the beautiful music, then I heard her again.

"Sam, search your heart for one of your profound memories and tell me what you see and what you feel."

I knew that her word choice of 'profound' meant what I would call, 'painful'. She wanted me to choose a memory that caused me suffering. It didn't take long.

Little Buddha Book Two

My whole world exploded into full view. I was sitting at the kitchen table. I was a young child and I was doing my homework. Ordinarily, my mom would be helping me, but today it was my father. I remember wishing it was her instead, because he had such a bad temper and he made me afraid and nervous. It was math homework and I wasn't very good at it, especially the more upset I felt.

I had just finished a set of problems and he was looking them over. I could see his face. It was starting to redden. I knew this was a bad sign and I knew it always led to his yelling at me.

"Good grief son, what's the matter with you?", he burst out. "We've been over these problems time and time again. You should know them by now. They're simple. I don't think you're even trying." He was winding up now. There would be a lot more before it was over.

"Really," he said. "I want you to tell me, what's wrong with you?" His voice had changed. It was loud and hard and a little bit scary.

"I want an answer!", he shouted.

I couldn't help it. I started to cry.

Little Buddha Book Two

"Don't be a baby," he yelled, "just answer my question."

I couldn't even remember his question. I felt so small, so unprotected. Where was my mom? Why wasn't she here. I wanted to disappear. To find a crack in the floor and crawl in and stay there for the rest of my life.

"I'm waiting," he growled. He was shaking now and his face was beet red. Finally, he threw the homework paper on the table and stomped out of the house.

I heard him say, "Useless kid," before the door slammed.

I fell apart. This wasn't the first time this had happened, but that didn't make it any better. This was not something I could 'get used to'. Nobody wants to have to get used to feeling like this. It's horrible.

Some part of me recognized I was in two places at the same time. One here, fully in this remembered experience and another, right here in this beautiful cottage with my Little Buddha. My mind was jumping back and forth. I felt so disjointed.

Little Buddha Book Two

Claire spoke, "Sam, I'm sorry he treated you like that. I know it hurt you and that the pain has never left you. I see that it waits for you and reappears in your life when certain events are challenging for you. But I want you to move back into your breathing, because we're not done with your journey."

I didn't like the idea that there was more. I wanted this to be over, I needed for this to be over.

But I trusted her and if she thought it was important for me to continue, I'd try. I shifted my attention to the music and slowly relaxed. I breathed deeply, in and out and listened for my heartbeat. I heard her breathing and followed along. After a few minutes, I was at peace.

"Okay Sam, look for the toggle switch."

I found it and Claire continued, "Now let's reconnect to your experience, when your father first spoke. When he said, "Good grief son, what's the matter with you?"

I saw him on the wall screen. I saw his whole mood change. Most of the time he was nice to

Little Buddha Book Two

me. We played together, throwing the football or baseball in the yard. We talked and went for ice cream. But then there were times like this. Times he'd just blow up.

"Sam, move the toggle switch toward your father."

As I did, a strange feeling came over me. I realized I'd shifted into what he was thinking and feeling. And the screen around the room changed. The picture was of him as a kid sitting in a classroom in school. The teacher was asking him a question and the whole class had turned to look at him, awaiting his answer.

I felt his nervousness. He didn't know the answer because he didn't even know she was talking to him. He'd drifted off again. It was so hard to pay attention, almost impossible. Everything distracted him.

He knew he was in trouble because this happened all of the time. His teachers face had a peculiar look on it. A kind of sneer, like she'd caught him again and was sort of happy about it.

"Henry, can you please tell me the answer?", she asked again.

Little Buddha Book Two

I felt my dad's sense of dread. He didn't know the answer or the question, but he knew it would be pointless to ask her to repeat it. He'd tried that before and all she would say was, "Oh, Henry, weren't you paying attention?"

Then all of the kids in the class would say, "Oh, Henry!" The teacher would tell them to stop, but my father knew she was secretly happy they were saying this, knowing it made him feel bad.

I sensed my father's shame. Shame at not being able to listen better. Shame at not being able to answer her questions, ever. And his shame turned to anger. How could a teacher treat him like this? Weren't teachers supposed to be nice to kids? And this made him even angrier.

I watched as my father reached out with his hand and grabbed a small book from his desk. I wondered what he was going to do. And then I watched as he threw it at his teacher once she'd turned her back to him. I watched as the book flew through the air and hit her square between her shoulder blades. Then the picture froze. Somehow, I knew everything that came after that. I knew how much trouble he was in. I knew that his parents, my grandparents, were

Little Buddha Book Two

going to punish him. And I knew how none of this would help him deal with his inability to pay attention or his anger about not being in control of his emotions. I didn't have to see all of the other events in his life to understand what drove him.

Before I'd seen this life experience of his, I didn't understand him at all. Now everything changed. I could see that he was replaying his own life as he tried to deal with me. I could feel his own sense of shame grow as he berated me for not being able to answer my math problems correctly. I felt awful for him. It must have hurt so badly to have that teacher treat him like that and then to have his parents discipline him instead of help him.

My own sense of anger and sadness about how he treated me started to evaporate. It was like some enormous weight had been lifted off me and I could breathe again. I felt such sorrow and compassion for my father and wished he could feel the release I was feeling, so remarkable, so glorious.

And there it was, the word Claire had used at the beginning of our conversation, glorious.

Little Buddha Book Two

"Sam," Claire said softly, "it's time to come back. Gently soften your breathing. Ease into your rhythm and when you're ready, open your eyes."

After a few minutes I could hear the music again and feel the chair I was sitting on. I realized I was hungry and thirsty. I opened my eyes and noticed the sun was back out. How beautiful.

"Is it always like that?", I asked.

"Like what?", she said.

"I don't know exactly. I guess I mean do you always see and feel the connection between events like that?"

"Not always," she responded, "but most of the time you do. Sometimes it takes longer because you need to follow the sequence of events through more people to be able to understand how you were affected. But this was pretty direct."

I was still trying to understand the fullness of the experience. I could certainly see that my suffering was an extension of my father's suffering and that it would have been pretty

Little Buddha Book Two

easy for me to have continued the pattern with people in my life. Actually, I'm sure I had.

I wondered if it was possible for me to break this chain? Could I accept that because my father was treated the way he was, that it was understandable that he treated me the way he did? I think I understood this intellectually, but I'm not sure I could emotionally accept it, because it still hurt, even knowing why.

"Claire, how can I let go of the pain I still feel?"

She smiled at me. "This is the glorious part Sam. You've just seen and felt what drove your father to act the way he did in his life, not just with you, but with everyone. You saw and sensed his shame and anger and you understand how it was not under his control. He had no skills to contain it or release it. He was a prisoner to his own feelings of unworthiness his whole life. If you'd moved the toggle switch to his teacher, you would have seen a similar pattern in her life. She'd been abused as a child and rather than have compassion for children, she had contempt, especially for the weak ones. You could follow the sense of pain and suffering they experienced far back into time. In fact, it's always present. And you know first-hand what

Little Buddha Book Two

this feels like and how incredibly powerful it is, and how you tend to believe there is no way out."

I did feel that and it was powerful. I wondered how Claire could use the word, 'glorious', as a label for this.

She knew what I was thinking. I could tell by looking at her. She smiled again and reached for my hand. I gave it to her and she spoke words I will always remember.

"Sam, I know this is difficult for you. It is for everyone. I know my answer is going to appear 'simple' to you and you'll question its value, but please try, because it's very important." She looked into my eyes and continued.

"Choice. That's the answer. To this and everything else in your life. It is the key to unlock any inner prison door. You've seen and felt what your father experienced. I'm not asking you to excuse his behavior. I know it caused you suffering and nothing can justify that. I know a part of you resents him for it, even knowing a part of his story. Can you see how your feelings make you a victim? How they make you a willing prisoner? How they

Little Buddha Book Two

inspire you to feel justified treating others poorly and without love?"

I did see and I did feel this. All of this. I didn't want to be incarcerated, stuck inside my own sense of guilt and shame and anger and unworthiness. I wanted out. I wanted to be free. I wanted Claire to give me the key to all of the doors that held me in place.

"Sam, the key you are looking for is 'free will'. It is your ability to make a choice. You can choose to forgive all those who have hurt you. You can choose to forgive yourself and feel true liberation. Sometimes you have to choose over and over again to make a new pattern, to alter your way of thinking and acting. You have to blaze a new trail and release your pain. You have the opportunity to choose happiness as a way of life. You can choose to celebrate, to love yourself and others and to know you are special, radiant and beautiful, exactly as you are."

I knew she spoke the truth. I also knew it might take me awhile to blaze the new trail she was suggesting. But I felt I could now. I felt I could release the pain I'd carried with me since childhood. I felt such a strong feeling of compassion for all those people that formed

Little Buddha Book Two

the chain reaction before it arrived inside of me. I wondered what it would have been like if Claire, my own little Buddha, had been able to tell each of them about this. Then I realized what was truly important was that she had just told me and now I could share that with others. How glorious!

Little Buddha Book Two

the nature of water

Little Buddha Book Two

"They're coming to lunch tomorrow," Claire said.

"Who's coming," I asked, wondering what she was up to now. I felt I lived in a constant state of surprise in her presence.

"We're having sort of an impromptu party because I was talking with June on the phone last night and she finally figured out my message and wants to see me in person." Claire seemed positively radiant as she continued, "Do you remember that I placed letters in the flower designs on the envelopes I sent you two years ago?"

"Sure," I said, "you told me it was some kind of code that June would recognize and would have fun trying to translate."

"That's right. Well, she's coming here because she thinks she knows what it means. I'm so excited to meet her in person. She should be here around 11:30 tomorrow morning. Can you come over early to help me set up?"

I nodded yes and said, "Sure, I'd be glad to, already wondering who else would be there.

Little Buddha Book Two

"How's she getting here?". I was curious because I knew June didn't like to drive very far since she'd fallen and injured her right leg.

"Maheer is going to bring her," Claire responded with an impish grin.

"Are you kidding me? It's over three hundred miles one way. Isn't that kind of far for a taxi ride" Wouldn't it be easier for her to fly and have Maheer pick her up from the airport?", I asked a little incredulously.

She looked at me but said nothing. Her eyes were soft and gentle and I knew I would get lost in them if I stared at her very long. There was something so special and mysterious about her. I could never figure it out. Then again, I didn't really try too hard, because I loved the mystery surrounding her. It definitely added to her charm, not that she needed any help with that.

"Actually Sam, it's three hundred thirty-three miles from her house to here".

There was that number again. That was the number of painted hearts we made and hung on her alley fence on the path to the beach.

Little Buddha Book Two

She'd told me it was an important number, but never why. And now here it was again.

"Okay Claire," I said, "what's so significant to you about the number 333?"

"Sam, certain numbers are almost magical to me. The number 333 represents the divine in action. Many cultures revere the number and when it shows up they feel very connected to their personal idea of god."

Claire sat and so did I. She stared off into the distance for a moment before saying more.

"To some, 333 represents the idea of trinity, where the divine is split into three, but each remains a part of the whole. I can truly appreciate what they see and what they believe. For me though, the significance is that 'three' stand for thought, word and action. It is this force that creates everything in our lives. Do you remember our conversation about karma?"

"Sure, I remember, but that was about 'intention', which I thought you said gave birth to thought, word and action." As usual I was a little confused. And I wondered what that had to do with the number three?

Little Buddha Book Two

"Yes," Claire said, "intention precedes thought, word and action. It actually gives each of them their creative energy. For me, three also stands for conceive, believe and act, which is another way of bringing things from the unseen to the seen. The repetition of the number three extends its power. It magnifies it."

"Okay," I said, "I'm sorry but I don't know where you're going with all of this. I understand that these concepts are really important and we've talked about them before, but what difference does the actual number make? Is every number important to you in its own way?"

I could see by the way that she was looking at me that she was amused. Even though she was only eleven, she had little laugh lines at the corners of her eyes. They intrigued me and right then I knew why. They were just like her mother's. There was something unique about both of their eyes, like they could see further. I don't mean distance, I mean depth. It's hard to explain, but it's like there was extra love and understanding in them, at least that's how they made me feel.

Little Buddha Book Two

"Yes, Sam every number has its own special meaning to me. It's not someone else's meaning though, it's the one I give it that matters to me. Do you realize that everything in our lives works this way? Can you see that nothing has an inherent meaning and that through our individual choice we establish our own personal meanings?"

I confess I had never really considered this. Was it true for me, I wondered? Was everything just 'neutral' until I gave it meaning? And then it dawned on me. I realized that I just accepted the meaning of things because that's the way I was taught. I realized how completely overwhelming it would have been if I'd had to decide what EVERYTHING in my life meant to me. It was far easier to accept what others had already decided and then told me.

But I think what Claire was saying to me was that I can, if I want to, if there is some value to me, choose my own personal meanings about everything. I really liked this idea. It felt completely liberating.

"So you feel the freedom to decide what everything in your life means to you?", I asked.

Little Buddha Book Two

"Yes, Sam. Being here gives me the freedom to create and experience this world any way I choose. One of the ways I do this is to attach personal significance to numbers and concepts, for instance, the number 333. And amazingly, once I do this, I find the concepts and numbers arrive in my life to reinforce the meanings. So, you see, I don't find it 'surprising' that June lives exactly 333 miles from here. Although not surprising, I do find it awesome."

I certainly had to agree. I was going to want to spend some more time with this whole idea. But, for now, I had some things to do. So, I said goodbye to Claire and promised to come back first thing in the morning. As I walked home I glanced at my watch. You guessed it, it was 3:33pm. Maybe there was something to this!

It's early the next day and I'm outside Claire's gate, peering into her backyard. I am amazed by the transformation. There is one set of long beautiful shimmering streamers running from the porch roof all the way to their back fence and another set running from the alley fence to the fence opposite. They're intricately interwoven and the sun is turning them into a wonderland. I don't know how they did this.

Little Buddha Book Two

What I do know it's one of the most amazing things I've ever seen.

I open the gate and walk through the yard and into their cottage.

"Good morning, Sunshine," shouts Claire from somewhere in the distance."

"Good morning, Starshine," I say in return. "How did you set up those streamers in the backyard?"

Claire bounced into the room and hugged me. "Mom and I did them last night. It's not as hard as you might think. We laid them all on the ground then wove them together and raised them up all at once and secured them. They look cool, don't they?"

"Yes," I said, "beyond cool, they look fantastic."

She smiled at me. The look on her face reminded me of a cartoon I'd seen as a child, the one where the cat has the canary in its mouth, but somehow is still able to grin.

"What?", I said. "knowing she wanted to tell me something more."

Little Buddha Book Two

Do they remind you of anything?", she asked.

"Not really," I responded. "Should they?"

She made a show of opening her mouth and blowing a little, like she was letting the canary out and then laughed. As usual she must have known about the cartoon I'd been thinking about. And then she laughed harder, a deep rolling laugh. I couldn't help it, even though it sort of felt like she was making a little fun of me, I laughed too.

Just then, Janine came into the room and looked at the two of us. And then she began laughing too. Some contagious things are pretty wonderful.

Finally, Claire caught her breath and said, "Sam, the streamers are like us, all interwoven, all amazing and beautiful and connected."

I hadn't thought about this when I'd first seen them but it was certainly true. We are all magnificent.

"Well, shall we start getting things set up before our friends arrive?', Janine asked.

Little Buddha Book Two

"Sounds great mom," Claire answered.

Later in the morning we heard a knock on the alleyway gate. Claire and I both went to see who it was. Actually, I'm pretty sure Claire already knew who it was, but she said nothing to me.

It was Gus from the paint store.

"Hello little princess," Gus said, "I guess I finally found you. There's certainly no mistaking this place. Your hearts are incredibly gorgeous and your yard is breathtaking. You sure put my paint to good use."

Claire pulled him through the gateway and hugged him. I saw him transform right before my eyes. It's hard to describe, but he seemed to glow.

"You know I already love you, don't you Gus?" Claire said, angling her head upward and gazing into his eyes.

"Yes," he answered, "I do, I really do. You are such a special child, girl, I mean young lady." He was obviously flustered. I knew she could have that effect on people.

Little Buddha Book Two

"Come in Gus," Claire said, "we're having a party and you're invited. Can you stay?"

"Sure, it's my day off from work and I'd love to stay, if that's really okay."

Claire beamed, "We already have a place set for you, so come with me."

I realized she was right, we'd set the table for six, even though I thought there would only be five of us. I wondered when I would cease to be surprised by her. Probably never. Actually, that was good with me because I loved her impromptu nature.

We'd just made our way into the cottage when we heard the sound of car doors being closed coming from the front yard. I opened the door and there stood June and Maheer.

"Welcome, come in," I said, while reaching out to hug June and shake Maheer's hand.

They both stepped in and Claire, Janine and Gus came into the entryway. Claire hugged them both and introduced everyone, then looking into our eyes, she said to each person, "I see you."

Little Buddha Book Two

Something always happened inside me when she said this. A kind of warmth spread through me. A special sense of being seen for who I was. I tried to release my usual way of interpreting intellectually what she might mean and just savor the feelings. I knew what it was. I felt deeply loved. I felt that Claire saw ME and loved ME. It was only three words, but so powerful.

I looked at the others gathered here and knew from their faces, that they felt it too. Funny, it dawned on me, it was THREE words. Maybe there was something to the importance she ascribed to numbers.

"Come on everyone, let's have some lunch," Claire said, leading us into the dining room.

It was really enjoyable and the conversation flowed easily from one topic to another. We'd each shared a few things about ourselves and everyone certainly seemed to be getting along well, especially June and Gus.

"Can I tell you a story," June asked?

"Absolutely," we all responded.

Little Buddha Book Two

"When I was a little girl, we lived in the middle of nowhere, in a very small town. My uncle Doug lived next door and he'd been in the Merchant Marine and traveled around the world several times. He ended up getting pretty sick and had to come back home to recuperate. I used to visit him all the time. I really loved him and thought he was the coolest person ever. He had such a great sense of humor and was fun to be around. One day, he brought out a box to show me. It was pretty big and at least for me, too heavy to move. He told me to open it and take a look inside. I did and couldn't believe my eyes. It was filled with post cards from all over the world. They were so beautiful and exotic to me and they had such an incredible variety of stamps on them. He said they were from friends he knew from his life. He told me they knew he couldn't travel anymore so they were going to travel for him and he could see the world through their eyes and their post cards."

June looked at each of our faces with a kind of dreamy expression and continued, "Well, I was totally fascinated by them and he could tell. He told me they were mine now, a gift from him. I was overwhelmed and pleased beyond belief. I felt like he'd just given me the whole world. I couldn't wait to take them home. It was then that he made a suggestion. He told me to take the map on the table next to me and, if it was okay with my mom, to hang it on my bedroom wall at home and then tack up the post cards and stretch a piece of yarn from the post cards to the place on the map that corresponded to it. I thought this was the most awesome idea ever. Because there were so many post cards, it took me over a month to accomplish. I would only take a few at a time, so I could visit him more often. He would tell me stories about his 'expeditions'. That's what he called them. That was the start for me. I was hooked. I wanted my own 'expeditions' and so when I was a junior in high school I went on my first foreign exchange program. I've been traveling ever since. I love learning about other cultures and experiencing firsthand what their lives are like. It's so different from here."

"That's incredible," I said. "So how many places have you been?"

"So far I've traveled around the world twice and visited over 105 countries and lived in eight of them."

"Wow," I said, truly amazed. "How did you afford all that travel?" I asked.

Little Buddha Book Two

June responded, "I was a teacher and pretty good with languages, so I could find work almost anywhere."

"I have so many questions I'd like to ask you about what you've seen and experienced. It's kind of hard to narrow them down," I stated.

"I have one," said Maheer, who'd been very quiet the whole time. "Did you ever travel through Lebanon?"

"No," June said, "it was too dangerous at the time that I was near there, but I'd always wanted to go there. Why, are you from there?"

I thought it was strange that they'd spent six or seven hours together in the car, I mean taxi, and they'd never talked about any of this. But I guess that's how it is sometimes, conversations just go in all different directions.

"Yes," Maheer said, but volunteered nothing more. It seemed to me that a special kind of sadness had overtaken him.

"I was a fisherman at one time," Gus said, bridging the gap in the conversation. "It's a surprisingly dangerous job. I remember one time we were fishing the Grand Banks and a

Little Buddha Book Two

wicked storm came up. Actually, we were getting sandwiched between two monster fronts. Like every fisherman or sailor, we'd been through lots of storms, but we'd always been okay. We had a great captain, a natural mariner. But this storm was different. I'd never seen him visually upset but he seemed unhinged and we were being literally tossed around like a toy. The waves were huge and the wind was ferocious. The whole crew was petrified and holding on for dear life. We knew we were in for a long haul and no one seemed to believe we were going to make it. Then one enormous wave hit us and I thought for sure we were going to flip over. It actually lifted us completely out of the water. In that moment something happened inside of me. It's like all of my fear was lifted out of me. My whole perspective shifted and I thought to myself, I'm acting as if I'm the boat, what if I see myself as the water? That's when it happened. All my fear blew away, carried off into the storm. I was the water and I had nothing to fear. Water moves, flows, crests, falls, but remains water. No fear. I could breathe again. In and out and easy. It's a transformation I've carried with me, even to this very day.

"That's an incredible story Gus," Claire said, "absolutely awesome."

Little Buddha Book Two

I agreed. I wondered though, how could I apply this to my life? How do you just decide to shift so radically, especially when you're in the middle of some chaos in your life? I needed to know more, so I asked Gus, "I think it's great you were able to find peace in the midst of that violent storm, but I can't imagine how you could do it. What's the secret?"

It seemed everyone wanted to know the same thing because everyone was looking directly at him.

Gus appeared a little thoughtful, perhaps trying to find the right words to explain about his shift. After a minute or two he spoke.

"There have been many times I've been afraid in my life, but that time was different, more extreme, I guess I'd say. The best I can tell you is that I felt my fear build and build to the point where I thought it would completely break me. In the past I would have fought it, but this time I gave in. It felt so much bigger than me. And in the act of giving in, it felt like an enormous wave had crashed over me and then it was gone and all of the fury was over. I felt peaceful and balanced, even though the storm continued all around me. And I knew everything would be okay. Not just in that

Little Buddha Book Two

moment, but in my whole life. The concept I carry with me is what I call, 'the nature of water', and it always brings me peace.

What a stunning idea, I thought. I wondered if there was a way for me to work this into how I viewed my life. I hoped so.

I looked around the table to see how what Gus had said was affecting others. It was then that I noticed that Maheer was crying. I saw Claire and Janine both reach out for his hands. Maheer was sobbing now, deep, racking, mournful sobs. I didn't know what to do to help him. What I saw was that Claire and Janine just sat with him and loved him, while he cried himself empty and dry. That was an important moment for me because I realized, you can't always fix everything. Some things are too powerful. And maybe, it's more about 'releasing' anyway. About letting go of what's being held so tightly. I thought about what Gus had said, about 'the nature of water'. About reaching that certain point where you give up and let go and stop fighting. I thought about him saying that he altered his whole awareness, from being in the boat, to being the water and how that took away his fear. Maybe that's what was happening to Maheer. Maybe his tears would give him freedom,

Little Buddha Book Two

liberating him from all the fears that bound him and would not let go. I sure hoped so.

We sat together in silence for a very long time. At last Maheer quieted and a look of utter peace spread across his face. He turned toward Gus and raised both his hands with his palms together, in a sort of prayer pose in front of him, then bowed his head.

"Thank you, my friend. Thank you for sharing your water story with me. I will remember it always. You are a good man and 'I see you'. Thank you."

Little Buddha Book Two

"I am…"

Little Buddha Book Two

"You know Claire sometimes I wonder who I am. At times I feel pretty sure and then something happens and everything shifts out of focus." I looked at her and she smiled at me. She seemed to have so many different smiles. Each had its own charm. The one she wore right now felt new to me and I wasn't sure what it meant.

"Sam, I think you've described how it is for everyone here," she said.

"But you don't ever seem to be, I don't know the right word, maybe 'unbalanced' is what I mean."

"That's the hard part for each of us. We always want to fill in all of the 'blanks' in our lives. You see me from the outside and you form an impression or draw a conclusion about what I'm thinking or what kind of mood I'm in, but you don't really know. At times, I'm not sure, so how could you know?"

She didn't say this in a challenging or unkind way, just sort of matter of fact. And she was right, of course. I made assumptions all the time about what others were thinking or feeling and then decided what actions to take or what words to say. It is a very reactive way to live

Little Buddha Book Two

your life. I told her all of this and her smile changed again. I recognized this one. It's the one she used when she had an idea for a project for me.

"It's a very challenging way to live your life when you're reactive to everything." She said, echoing me. "Trying to decide what course of action to take based on a set of most likely 'false assumptions', is an unsure way to exist. Does it make you feel like you are always guessing?"

"Yes, and often I guess wrong," I responded.

"Would you like to try a different approach?" she asked.

I wondered what she had in mind. I have to say all of her suggestions were worth pursuing so I said, "Yes, absolutely."

"What I have in mind comes in parts. How you answer will determine the number of parts, but please understand this is not a test where there are 'right' and 'wrong' answers. There are just 'your' answers."

"I understand," I said, "how do I get started?"

Little Buddha Book Two

She grinned at me. I'd seen this grin before too. It usually meant that I'd be sitting in my cottage looking out at the ocean tonight for a long time.

"I'd like you to find a new notebook and open to the first page, then number the lines from one to one hundred. At the top of the page write the words "I AM A" followed by three dots. The idea is that you write down one hundred answers to that simple question. The answers can be anything."

Claire looked at me to see my reaction. It seemed like a pretty simple task and I was wondering if there was a catch to it.

She laughed, looked into my eyes and said, "No, Sam, there's no catch. You just write one hundred answers and bring it back tomorrow, or the next day, if you need more time."

For about the millionth time I wondered how she was able to read my mind. Well, I had a project to do, so I said goodbye, hugged her and walked back to my cottage.

It didn't seem like this would be very hard, but I never really knew until I got started. I also had

Little Buddha Book Two

to remember she said this was only the first part.

It took me about two hours to complete. I'd have a spurt and write down a bunch of answers at one time and then nothing. I'd have to alter my thinking a bit and then another set of answers would come. I found the easiest were, I guess I'd call them 'relationships'. Who was I in relation to others; son, brother, boss, coworker. Then there were things I did; bowler, canoer, reader, writer, food lover. I began to realize that my answers fell into line with what she'd described to me as my 'human make up', because I have physical, emotional, mental and spiritual parts. I looked over my list to see where my answers fit. I wondered what Claire's answers would be and how they'd compare to mine.

It's the next morning and I've devised a new plan to surprise her. I don't know how she always knows when I'll arrive but she does. It is mind boggling to me and a bit unnerving, although I don't know why I really care.

I decided to call Maheer for a ride because she'd never expect me to show up in his taxi. He said he'd be happy to give me a ride, as

Little Buddha Book Two

long as he got to see Claire and Janine in the process.

Maheer picked me up and it only took a few minutes to drive to Claire's cottage. We walked up her front path and knocked on the door. I heard pounding footsteps and then the front door swung open.

"Wow, what a surprise," Claire exclaimed, "it's so nice to see you both."

She couldn't fool me. She was a great little actress when she was clowning around, but I could tell, she knew it was us before she opened the door. Again, I wondered, how was it possible for her to always know? I felt a real sense of ambivalence about actually knowing how she did it. I guess I kind of liked the 'mystery' of it. She was my very own magician, just one more of her special charms.

"So good to 'see you' my precious one," Maheer said. "I can only stay for a few minutes because I have another fare to pick up." He hugged Claire and asked, "Is your mom at home?"

"She's in the kitchen and I'm sure she'd love to see you."

Little Buddha Book Two

Maheer headed off to find Janine as Claire and I went out to the back patio. The shimmering streamers were still there and still glorious.

"So how did it go?" she asked.

"Great," I said, "all done. It wasn't as hard as most of your projects. You must be slipping." I knew that wasn't a wise thing to say, as soon as it left my mouth.

A grin jumped onto her face.

'Oh no' I thought, here we go.

"Okay Sam, here's part two. Turn the page in your notebook and start a new list and number it from one to one hundred and write, 'I AM' and three dots at the top."

"That sounds like pretty much what I've already done," I said.

She titled her head and gazed at me. "I think you'll find that this will be a very different list with the 'A' missing from the end."

I sat with that statement for a minute and saw what she meant. There was a big difference

Little Buddha Book Two

between, 'I AM A...' and 'I AM...'. This was going to be more 'personal'. I'd have to see when I started working on it, but it felt much more challenging. I guess I'd find out later tonight.

We had a great day together. We swam in the salty ocean, did an art project, ate and talked and took a long nap. I loved spending time with Claire and Janine. When I was with them, everything felt right with the world. I wondered what I brought to the table for them. I immediately realized that 'feeling' belonged on my list, 'I AM INSECURE'. This part of her project was sure to be interesting.

It's later and I'm home sitting at my kitchen table staring out at the ocean. I am so fortunate to be able to come here every summer. I thought to myself, what a great way to start my list, so I wrote, 'I AM FORTUNATE'.

Filling out the list was very similar to last night. I'd think of a series of answers then run out of steam. I'd sit back and then more would pop out. Knowing a lot of adjectives was certainly coming in handy.

When I was done, I was surprised by my answers. They were overwhelmingly 'positive'.

Little Buddha Book Two

I knew that Claire had cautioned me about 'labeling', but I'd completed my assignment and was doing a simple review of my answers. Whatever message they meant to send me, I didn't think would be adversely affected by evaluating whether they were generally 'positive' or 'negative' words. I'd have to ask her about that when I saw her.

I was pretty sure that if I'd done this assignment a few years ago or even as recently as last year, my answers wouldn't have been as kind and loving as they were. Claire and Janine had such a profound effect on me. I guess I'm back to where I started…'I AM FORTUNATE'.

It's the morning now and I've taken another route to her cottage, coming up her alleyway from the beach. I have no doubt she already knows this. I wonder if 'clairvoyant' is on her list. I laugh a little to myself thinking how many 'claire' words applied to her.

I open her gate and cross the yard. She's standing in the doorway and looking in my direction.

"Hello my divine friend," she said, "how are you this morning?"

Little Buddha Book Two

"I AM AMUSED," I said, wondering if she knew that 'DIVINE' was the second word on my list. Of course, she did.

She and I went inside her cottage. We hugged and then I stood still, waiting for her to ask me how I did with her assignment. She didn't ask. Instead, she put her hands on my shoulders, stood on her tiptoes, looked directly into my eyes and said, "I see you, my brother."

A warmth spread through me and one more list answer came to me, 'I AM SEEN'. It still felt so good to be seen.

"Thank you for the assignment," I told her, "it was eye opening to me."

"Really," she responded, "in what way?"

"When I looked over my list I noticed how many wonderful words there were on it. I believe you and your mom deserve most of the credit for that. You've both taught me so much and I am so grateful to you."

"Sam, it's our pleasure. You are our pleasure."

Little Buddha Book Two

We talked some more about my 'answers', then Claire asked me if I was ready for part three.

"Sure, but where are we going with this?" I asked, wanting to have some sense of our direction.

"Do you remember what you said to me the other day that started this project?" she asked.

"Sure," I said, "I told you that sometimes I wonder who I am."

"That's right," she said, "and now you've created two hundred answers to the question. So how do you feel about it now?"

I'm sure she'd used the word 'feel' deliberately. Whenever we were doing a project, she'd always shift my focus to my feelings.

"I guess it's a bit clearer, but maybe I'm asking the wrong question for what I want to know." I couldn't quite put my finger on what I was after.

It seemed to me that she understood my dilemma because she asked me a question that brought more focus.

Little Buddha Book Two

"Do you mean, 'who you are' or 'why you're here on this earth at this time'?"

In my mind the two questions were intimately related. To decide 'who I was', I felt it was also important to know 'why I was here'. Even having some insight now to who I felt I was didn't answer the question of why I was here.

So, I asked, "Claire, why am I here?" I really wanted to know. I needed to know. I hoped she would take pity on me and for once, not ask me anything else. I wanted her to just answer me.

Claire sat down and closed her eyes. Her breathing slowed and she hummed quietly. I watched her visibly relax. She was so beautiful. I wondered how she would look when she was older. At that moment, Janine passed through the room and I knew what Claire would look like. She'd look a lot like her mom. And if it was possible, she'd be even more beautiful than she was right now.

Claire was radiating her peace into the room and into me. I closed my eyes and breathed in and out, slow and steady. It still amazed me how much this changed my whole perspective

Little Buddha Book Two

about things. After a while she touched my knee and asked me to open my eyes. I have no idea how long we'd been sitting there, but I also knew it didn't matter to me.

"Sam, you've heard about the 'afterlife' haven't you?"

"Yes," I responded. "it's been a fascination of mine for a long time."

Claire studied me. "For you to understand the 'afterlife' and your present 'earth life', it's important that you understand the 'before life'. It's all a matter of perspective."

I wondered what she meant by the 'before life'. I'd never heard anyone talk about that.

"What do you mean," I asked.

"We've touched on this before, but not in the same context. There are some wonderful teachers in this world. Here's what one of them told me. Before you came here to earth, you were a part of the ocean of love. You existed in a state of bliss. Everything was perfect. And yet the essence that is you, chose to leave so that you could come here to earth. You did this in order to 'experience' every possibility. You

Little Buddha Book Two

did this so you could create and experience all things. So that you could KNOW joy and heartache, pain and pleasure, despair and dreams. Before you came here you knew only peace and love. You could not 'feel' the full range of physical, emotional and mental experiences because you 'knew the truth'. The truth that there is only love. You came to earth world to understand all opposites, knowing that one day you would want to remember the truth of who you really are. So, your journey here is filled with opportunities. Your ability to create and experience whatever you desire is limitless."

Claire gazed at me. In her eyes I saw something new, and yet something I fully recognized. A familiar 'light'. Somehow, I knew that she and I had always known each other. It's hard for me to explain, but I felt a 'kinship' with her. From her expression I believe she felt the same thing.

"Claire, I think I understand about coming here to experience the range of things. And within those experiences I have the free will to choose. No one is controlling my every move. Every decision is mine and based on my choices, I can create my own experience of this earth life. Is that what you're telling me?"

Little Buddha Book Two

"Yes, Sam. Your very earth nature provides you with unlimited dreams."

"Can one of those dreams be for me to know who I am and why I am here?" I think we'd finally arrived at part three of her assignment.

"Yes, Sam. What others have taught me is that the answers to these questions depends on the actions 'you' take. Each of your choices and decisions proclaims who you are and why you are here."

I had one more question. "So, what did you mean when you said that one day I would want to 'remember the truth' of who I am?"

"Because Sam, everyone wants this. They may not be aware of it consciously, but deep inside of them they know there is a space waiting to be filled and they know only one thing can fill it. They sense this and they search so hard and so long and yet never seem to come any closer. They try to fill it with things of this world, but none can answer this deep desire."

I believe I knew what she was talking about. Earlier in my life I think I tried a few of these

Little Buddha Book Two

solutions. She was right of course, none of them ever worked.

"So, Claire, what's the answer? What will fill this open space inside of us?" I desperately wanted to know.

"Love," she said. "Remembering what it is like in the 'before life', when we were all a part of the ocean of love."

Somehow, I knew that would be the answer. But at the same time, I wondered, how can we 'remember'? How can we be connected to the source of love so we can live filled and complete?

She must have known what I was thinking because she came over to me and hugged me. I understood. I felt touched by her love. I felt her heart beat inside of me. I knew it was in her 'action' that I felt filled by love. She 'intended' to give me love, freely and completely. I could do the same, to her and to everyone I choose. How they accepted it was their choice, but I could send love, give love, feel love anytime or all of the time. That was how to remember.

Little Buddha Book Two

I had one more word to add to my assignment,
'I AM LOVE.'

Little Buddha Book Two

String theory

Little Buddha Book Two

String theory

"Good morning Claire," I said as I came through the gate.

Claire was lying in one of their comfortable lawn chairs that reclined, watching a cat that was stalking something in her backyard. I'd never seen the cat before. She was a very pretty calico. She was so focused on her quarry that nothing else seemed to matter.

"Good morning sunshine," Claire whispered, "it's so nice to see you."

"It's so nice to be seen," I said. "Whose cat is that?", I asked.

"It's my friend Jamie's new cat," Claire responded, "isn't she beautiful?"

I'm more a of dog person, but I could certainly agree, she was extraordinary.

"You know she's hunting, right?" I asked. It had always sort of bothered me that it seemed that cats hunted for sport. After all, if they were a house cat like this one, they didn't need to hunt to eat and it seemed harsh and unnecessary for them to kill.

Little Buddha Book Two

Claire turned toward me and her expression changed. She had a curious look on her face as she studied me. I wasn't sure what she was looking for.

"She's living her nature Sam. You do realize that, don't you?"

Maybe some part of me did, but it still troubled me that she was going to kill another animal and then just walk away, like it meant nothing. That wasn't a part of nature that I liked.

"Sam, each essence on earth has a 'nature' and she is following hers. It's a part of her core. You're doing the same thing. You're acting and thinking according to patterns you've been taught and patterns you aren't even sure where they came from. They just seem 'second nature' to you." She waited a moment and then continued, "You've decided how a cat should behave according to principles that feel 'right' to you. She's not thinking and evaluating. She hasn't created a world of comparisons and relationships. She just knows it's important to hunt. It's part of who she is."

I did know this, but I still didn't like it.

Little Buddha Book Two

"Sam, why does it challenge you?" Claire's voice was soft and there was no edge to it. It was clear that she wasn't upset with me, she just wanted to know why I felt the way I did.

"I'm not really sure," I said, "but it's always bothered me. I guess maybe it reminds me that I do the same thing sometimes."

Claire smiled at me and asked, "What do you mean?"

"Sometimes I act without thinking about what I'm doing. I have some goal and pursue it and I never stop to consider the outcome, other than it's what I want. Often, when I do this I hurt someone or end up feeling really bad about myself. I guess the cat reminds me of this. I pursue my quarry, my prey, my desire without regard for anything else, even though I'm already well fed."

Until that moment and Claire's question I don't think I ever realized the truth of this. I didn't like that part of me and I blamed myself for it, the same way I was blaming the cat."

Claire looked at me with such compassion. "I understand Sam. We all follow our nature. It's part of living here. It's not 'right' or 'wrong' in and of itself. It's important to recognize though we're not bound to it. We can see it and make a different choice about it. That's a beautiful thing."

"That's one of the things I love about you Claire, you can always see the bright side. What would I do without you?"

She beamed at me and reached out her hand. I took it and felt a surge of energy. What a wonderful part of her nature, to give off such a beautiful and amazing love with a simple, single touch.

"How about a glass of iced tea?", she asked.

"Sound great," I said, as we headed inside.

As she opened the screen door to her cottage, the cat raced between her legs and sprinted inside. Claire laughed and turned back toward me.

"She must be pretty thirsty too. I wonder if she prefers milk or iced tea?"

Little Buddha Book Two

I was curious if the cat was following more of its nature or just liked the challenge of running through obstacles, in this case, Claire's legs.

Claire poured me a glass and then one for herself and put down a saucer of milk on the floor for the cat.

"What's the cat's name?", I asked.

"Schrodinger," Claire answered.

"You've got to be kidding," I responded. "Who names their cat, Schrodinger?" I had a vague recollection of having heard the name before, but I couldn't place it.

"My friend Jamie's father named her. He's a scientist and he thought it was a really funny name for a cat. I'm sure Jamie will be by soon looking for her."

I'd never heard about Jamie before. Claire was full of surprises. I'd known her now for five years and it seemed there was always something new to discover about her and her world.

"How do you know her?", I asked.

Little Buddha Book Two

"We're homeschool buddies," Claire responded, "have been for the past three years. She's one of my best friends and she just moved here last week. They're still getting settled."

As if on cue, we heard a knock on the back door.

"Come in Jamie," Claire yelled.

As she walked in I was immediately aware of something, but I couldn't define it. The best I could explain was that she had an amazing aura and a wonderful vibration. I felt it was no wonder that she and Claire were best friends.

"Hey Claire," Jamie said, "have you seen Schrodinger?"

Claire glanced over at me and closed and pointed to her eyes. Somehow, I got the message, Jamie was blind. I guess this accounted for her not seeing the cat in the kitchen or me, standing right next to Claire.

"Wait a minute," Jamie said, "do you have a guest? I'm sorry, am I interrupting?"

Little Buddha Book Two

"Not at all, Jam. This is Sam, my very own ray of sunshine."

Jamie held out her hand for me to shake. As I extended my hand, she quickly pulled hers back. I was really surprised and wondered what was happening.

Jamie and Claire howled with laughter. Apparently, this was some kind of running joke between them.

Jamie stopped laughing after a few moments, held out her hand again and said, "It's great to finally meet you Sam."

This time she let me shake her hand. It was incredibly soft and warm.

Claire looked at me and explained, "That's how we met. Jamie did the same thing to me. I thought it was so funny at the time. I guess I still do."

Jamie spoke up, "You see Sam, I need to do something to change the dynamic because when people first meet me all they see is a blind girl. I'm more than that, so I create an immediate shift in our relationship. I want them to know that I'm fun and interesting, which I

Little Buddha Book Two

am. Sometimes they think I'm rude. That's still better than them pitying me."

I saw her point.

"Well I can see why the two of you are friends," I said. "Jamie, can I ask you something?"

"Sure, shoot," Jamie responded.

"Is there some significance to your cat's name? I know I've heard it before, but I can't come up with the reference."

She smiled and shook her head from side to side. "You'd have to know my dad," she said. "He's a quantum physicist and the reference is to a very famous cat that belonged to scientist. It has something to do with a 'thought experiment' he once did and how random subatomic particles act, but I can't tell you much more than that."

At that moment, we heard a crash in the living room. Actually, it sounded like several things had fallen on the floor. We all went to see. There, laying on the floor on her back was Schrodinger. She had yarn wound around both front paws and was kicking her back legs, trying to unwind it. Obviously, the yarn had

Little Buddha Book Two

been connected somehow to several things on the living room table and they'd all fallen as she'd pulled the yarn.

Claire started to laugh and explained to Jamie what had happened.

"What a great 'object lesson' you're teaching us Schrodinger. Thank you," Claire said while reaching down to untangle the cat.

"What are you talking about Claire?", I asked.

"Sam, tell me what you see and what you think happened."

This seemed like a pretty silly question to me, but then I remembered practically nothing was simple to Claire. I was a little wary as I answered.

"It appears that our feline friend tugged on the yarn which was somehow connected to some things on the table and when she pulled hard enough, they all crashed to the floor."

Claire clapped and said, "Very good. Can you tell me what the "object lesson" is?"

Little Buddha Book Two

We'd had lots of conversations about object lessons before, but I rarely saw what she did. She told me they were when an event in life illustrates a grand principle and this principle could teach us things and offer us insight. She said the more we paid attention, the faster we'd 'remember'. Actually, she said it a lot.

Okay, I thought, I'll keep this simple; cat pulls yarn, yarn connected to stuff, stuff falls on the floor. Obviously, I was missing something.

Jamie spoke, "Claire is it okay if I give it a try? I don't want to steal Sam's thunder, but I have an idea."

Claire looked at me questioningly and I said, "go for it Jamie."

"Well because I've spent so much time in my father's world, one explanation could be that it's a representation of string theory and the connection between objects, especially objects in motion. He's told me that most scientists now believe that all tiny molecules are made up not only of atoms, which have electrons, protons and neutrons, but there are even smaller particles inside. They're known as quarks. Some scientists believe that inside of a quark there is a vibrating string of energy,

Little Buddha Book Two

which moves at different frequencies. So my theory for the object lesson is that my cat, the yarn and the stuff connected to the yarn are all moving in some grand scheme, set in motion by pulling on the yarn."

My first thought was, oh man, I wished I'd been homeschooled. These kids knew way more than I did. Even now I was awed. My second thought was I hoped the answer was easier than that.

Claire said, "That's beautiful Jam, but I had something else in mind."

Jamie tilted her head and smiled in Claire's direction, then said to me, "It's up to you Sam, my man."

I decided to keep it simple, "In life there are often 'threads' that are connected and when you pull on them a lot of stuff may surface and some of the stuff may crash down on you."

Claire grinned, "Also true, but also not what I had in mind. It's not that either of you are 'wrong', because you both know there is no 'wrong' answer. My take away is that this represents how life unravels to show us the truth. Schrodinger was curious about the yarn.

Little Buddha Book Two

She didn't realize it was connected to anything, she just wanted to play. As she pulled the yarn harder and harder, everything connected to it inched closer to the table edge, until all at once, it fell to the floor.

Jamie and I waited patiently for Claire to continue.

"We all do the same thing all the time," Claire said, "we have lots and lots of loose threads in our lives, like unanswered questions and unsolved problems. Sometimes when we pull on the threads, what we discover surprises us. And sometimes we don't realize what's going to happen as we keep pulling and it turns out that something falls on us. It can seem unexpected and unpleasant. And sometimes we need others help to untangle ourselves."

"I like it," Jamie said enthusiastically. "So, if I continue pulling this thread with you, we can find meanings if we're paying attention BEFORE things crash to the floor."

"Yes," responded Claire. It takes practice to see what was previously unseen, but it's so worth the time."

Little Buddha Book Two

Claire glanced over at me and smiled. "You want an example don't you Sam?"

"I guess that's a part of my nature Claire. Yes, please," I said.

"Sam, several years ago mom and I were talking about how we viewed our lives. She told me that she'd discovered a way to pull a great deal of meaning from her loose threads. She created what she calls a 'celebration journal'. I already have lots of entries in mine."

I admit I was very intrigued, especially since it was a practice her mother, Janine used. Although I'd know Janine for quite a while, I don't think I knew anything about her practices."

"Claire, I'd love to know more. Can you give me a sense of how it works?"

"Of course," she said. "I have to set the stage a little. It's called a celebration journal on purpose because my mom views every part of life as a celebration. She believes that everything will ultimately work toward her good. It will all help her remember the truth. So, it doesn't matter to her how an event, a thread, first appears. It may seem to others as

Little Buddha Book Two

a 'negative' event, but mom knows there is always more to everything. She knows that for whatever appearance of 'negative' there is an equal or greater 'positive' at the end of every thread."

"I think I understand the principle you're talking about, but can you explain how it works practically speaking, because I'm not sure I get it yet?"

I looked over to Jamie to see her reaction. She was smiling broadly. I guess she'd already made the connection. I guess that's alright, it just takes me a little longer.

"Here's one you'll remember Sam. Do you recall when I was eight years old and had cancer?"

Of course, I remembered. I was really scared for her and for me too. I'd just found her after two years of searching and I didn't want to lose her again. I nodded to her and she continued.

"At first I 'labeled' the disease as 'very bad'. I thought to myself, is this it, is this all the time I'm going to be here? I wondered about all of the pain and how I would manage it. I was afraid for my mom and worried about what my

Little Buddha Book Two

disease would do to her, what my death would do to her. I wondered why this was happening to me and what I would need to do to get better. Could I even get better?"

Claire's face looked calm and peaceful as she recounted this challenging time in her life. I don't believe I could ever be peaceful about this. Even my recollections about watching her go through the experience made me upset.

"Sam, I want you to do something for me."

"Okay," I said.

"I want you to close your eyes and gently breathe, slowly in and out."

I did as she requested and I felt a peaceful feeling grow in me. Some part of me knew why she was asking me to do this. I needed to be able to fully listen. When my breathing was even and my body relaxed, she started speaking.

"You see Sam, I needed to feel all of my feelings first. My mom taught me that if you don't, they will all become loose threads and there is no telling when they will unravel. By feeling your true feelings, your life becomes

Little Buddha Book Two

woven together and your fabric is strong. This was the first GIFT for me to celebrate about having the challenge of cancer. But this same concept applies to everything we experience in life."

I knew this to be true. I knew because I was on day number 1069 of my 'feelings journal'. That's the notebook I write in every single day to share my feelings with myself. I explore my inside world and see if I would benefit from taking any actions. If a feeling comes up, I see what direction it seems to suggest and then I take it. Action becomes very important. I guess that's a pretty big GIFT I've received from my feelings journal practice.

I'm starting to get what she's saying, but I still wanted to know more. I asked her to continue.

"Sam, as I was going through my treatments, I began writing down everything I was experiencing. I tried to be 'neutral' about the way I phrased things, to give myself time to find the messages inside the experience. That turned out to be another huge GIFT. I found that 'just being with my disease' instead of 'fighting it', allowed me SPACE. I found that as I sat still, insights came to me. I came to an understanding within me that my disease was

Little Buddha Book Two

not happening TO me, rather it was happening THROUGH me. Many of the patients I met during my treatments felt as though they were the victims. They felt that they were being punished, sometimes justly, but most of the time, unjustly. They were angry with the world or with god or with everyone and they had so many loose threads to deal with."

I interrupted so I could get clarification, "But you didn't feel that way?"

"At first, I wondered, but Michael helped me shift my awareness."

I love Michael, her cousin, and I was so in awe of his wisdom. In the future I hoped to spend part of the summer with him.

"How did Michael help you?" I asked.

"It's a little bit hard to explain," Claire responded, "because it's something you FEEL, rather than something you THINK."

Claire asked me to extend my arms in front of me, with my left palm facing up and my right palm facing down. She did the same so that our palms faced each other and there was about an inch or two of space between them.

Little Buddha Book Two

She asked me to focus my attention on the space between our palms. As I did, I felt a strong vibrating energy. It felt good. There was a kind of humming to it and it grew stronger the longer it went on.

"Sam, this is the energetic force of the universe that we're holding and it is present all the time."

It felt awesome and I asked Claire, "Did you use this to get better?"

"Yes, Sam, this was a part of it. Every day I would hold my hands over my heart and focus and feel the energy of the universe moving through me. I aligned with the way the energy was moving and realized I was a part of the process. I realized that everything is in constant motion. I realized that if I felt my disease was happening TO me, it made the energy static. It came and then stopped inside me and the more I resisted, the worse I felt. Michael encouraged me to shift and allow the energy to move THROUGH me. As soon as I did this, everything changed. I felt like I was a part of the process and I stop resisting. I felt everything flow through me. Oh Sam, this was such an important GIFT to me. I don't know how long it would have taken for me to realize this, had I not experienced that disease. I believe I would eventually have learned this, but because it happened when I was eight, my whole life since then has been so meaningful and special."

I was totally blown away. I could not have imagined that anyone could make such an enormous shift and recognize so many gifts. I admired and loved her so much.

Right at that moment we heard another crash, this time from the kitchen. I wondered what object lesson Schrodinger had in mind for us this time.

Little Buddha Book Two

sparks

Little Buddha Book Two

It's the last week of the summer and Claire wants to do one more project. She wants to string lights around the painted wooden hearts hanging on the alleyway fence. I love the idea and can't wait to get started.

"Where are the lights?", I ask.

Claire tells me they are in the hall closet, which happens to be opposite the downstairs bathroom door.

I walk down the hall and notice the bathroom door is open and steam is pouring out. Billowing would be a better description. Wow, Janine must have taken a really hot shower. I open the closet door and search through the shelves until I come to a box labeled, 'outside lights'. I pick it up and turn to catch up with Claire, who has already headed outside. That's when I notice the bathroom window. It's completely steamed over, except for a perfectly shaped heart with two letters right in the middle of it. They're not letters I would have expected and they form a word I also would not have expected. There, written in cursive, is the word, 'ME'.

I know Janine must have done it, since she's the only other one here today besides Claire

Little Buddha Book Two

and me. I wonder, what does it mean? I can't imagine myself putting 'ME' in the middle of my own heart.

Janine is so different from anyone I've ever met before. I thought Claire was amazing, and of course she is, but then I realize that Janine must be even more amazing, since she is Claire's teacher. It occurred to me that I was 'labeling' again. I'd come to understand that it didn't matter if I labeled something 'good' or 'bad', it always prevented me from seeing clearly what was evident if I stayed open and attentive and clear.

After Claire and I put the lights up, we decided it was time for lunch. We were going to wait until dark before we turned them on, so we could get the full effect.

As we were setting out plates, silverware and glasses, we heard a loud 'thump'. We looked at each other and both said at the same time, "Schrodinger's here". Yup, we saw her running around the backyard. She must have jumped to the top of the fence and thumped down into the yard. She was really fun to watch.

A few moments later Jamie walked in through the gate and called out to us.

Little Buddha Book Two

"Am I in time for lunch?"

"Perfect timing," Claire answered, "come in and sit down and tell me what you'd like."

Janine joined us and we all sat watching Schrodinger's latest antics. After unsuccessfully trying to catch a few bugs, she decided to come in and lie down on the dining room carpet. I thought she might be content to rest for a while, but no, she started to stalk several sun spots on the carpet, as they moved around the room. Every once in a while, she would pounce on one and try to scratch it or pick it up, never realizing it was not something 'on' the carpet, but a light cast there by the sun. I had to admit, she certainly was an entertaining cat.

After we finished lunch, Claire, Jamie and Schrodinger decided to go for a walk on the beach. Claire invited me, but I declined. I wanted to talk with Janine and this was the perfect opportunity.

Once they left, I turned toward Janine and said, "Can I ask you something?"

"Anything you want, Sunshine," Janine replied.

Little Buddha Book Two

"Can you tell me about the heart on the bathroom window?"

"So, you noticed that huh? Well I thought you might. What do you want to know?"

"Have you always done it? What does it mean? Is it the word, 'ME' or does it stand for something else?" As usual, I was full of questions.

"Actually, Sam, the answer is really simple. Many years ago, I went out west on a vision quest. Incredible things happened to me, the most important of which was that I came to fully accept and embrace that I love myself. It took me a long time, but once it happened, I wanted to remind myself every day. The heart on the window is one of my reminders."

I had a lot more questions now, but that's how it always was with Claire and Janine. As one question was answered several more questions arose. I could tell she knew this was what I was thinking. I tried to narrow my questions down. What did I really, truly want to know? And then I had it.

Little Buddha Book Two

"You absolutely, totally, completely love yourself?" I asked, wondering if this was possible. In their care, I had come to respect and value myself, I recognized I was a good person, a very good person. I knew I meant something to others. I was generous and fair and caring. But, did I love myself? I couldn't answer this question with her level of truth and certainty.

"I do," she said, "I know it in my 'knower', that place inside me where the truth always resides and no doubt lingers."

I wanted that. More than anything, I wanted that.

"How did you find this place? How did you stay there long enough to come to believe in your love for yourself," I asked, sounding a bit like I was pleading, which I suppose I was.

"Sam, I want to tell you something very important. We'll get to my actual answers, but we would benefit from some exploring first." She stretched out her arms toward me with her left palm facing up and her right palm facing down and said, "Put out your arms and place your hands the same way as mine and grasp my hands lightly in yours."

Little Buddha Book Two

I did. There was an immediate energetic force, like a circuit had been completed.

"Wow," I exclaimed, "what is that?"

"That's the vibration of the universe," she said, "isn't it divine?"

We held hands like this for a few minutes. I felt 'transported'. That's the only word I can think of to describe it.

"Now take your hands and hold them over your heart and bring your attention to that space inside you, to your inner heart."

I did. I'd never felt anything like this. I'd felt a lot of different sensations during Janine and Claire's guided meditations, but nothing remotely like this. The energy was so radiant and magnificent and it was all directed inward, into me. And I realized that's what made this so different. It was so personal and so incredibly important. She'd started the energy flow, but now this was all about me. The love I felt for me.

I wanted to stay right here forever. I have no idea how long I experienced this. But

Little Buddha Book Two

eventually I became aware of being 'present'. I knew without question what design I'd be making on my steamy bathroom window from now on. I wasn't naïve enough to think I would always feel this way, but I could always remind myself and draw my own attention to this piece of my truth, to the heart of me.

"Thank you so much Janine," I said, while bowing to her.

"You're very welcome, Sam."

"Can I ask you another question?"

"Of course, what do you want to know?"

Janine was calm and so beautiful. At that moment I realized why this was true. A part of her beauty came from her own self-love. Somehow it magnified her physical beauty. She was truly awesome.

"What else did you experience on your vision quest?" I'd heard about them for several years, but still felt I didn't really understand.

"Everyone's experience is different, unique to them, unique for you. Someday you'll know this first hand, but for now I'll share a bit of

Little Buddha Book Two

mine with you. For most, there is a sense of what is coming before they start their journey. It helps them to be prepared. Once they start, they come to see and feel a presence with them. That's how it was with me.

She seemed to go into a trance, recalling her quest and she seemed so peaceful, so tranquil.

Janine spoke, "It was the first time I ever asked a spirit guide to come and be with me. I'd thought they would come when I was 'ready' and not before, so I never thought to ask. But as I sat, peaceful and still, releasing my 'control' and opening, I asked for my spirit sister to come and be with me. To love and guide me and share her truth with me. And she did come. I remember it, as if it's happening right in this moment. It's so clear and vivid."

Janine stopped speaking for a few minutes and closed her eyes. I sat wondering what her spirit sister had told her, what truths she shared that changed the way Janine lived, the way she loved. I wondered too, when would I get a chance to go on a vision quest?

Janine's eyes opened. They were perfectly clear and looked so alive. "Sam, my spirit

Little Buddha Book Two

guides name is Lia. It's her name and also an acronym, because it stands for 'Love In Action'." Janine looked around the room and then her gaze settled on me. "Sam, as soon as I felt her presence, I knew she loved me and wanted to help me create my most meaningful life. She asked me to trust her. She told me it was her greatest desire to show her love for me through her actions. She wanted me to know, that she wanted what I wanted or something even better. She told me this was and would always be the case. She asked me to be open to her help and support and guidance. She said she would never choose for me, but she would always point the way toward the light. She asked me to be patient and to rely on her. She knows that it is hard for humans to give up their sense of control. She knows that we appear to want what we want, when we want it, not realizing that might not be what serves us most. She explained that we often judge by immediate appearances, so we think that we don't receive the right outcomes. She said that this is where patience was important, because often our greatest good takes some time to appear. She asked me to release any sort of labeling of experiences so that I could stay present. Present and attentive to all of the message that my experiences were here to share with me. She asked me to

Little Buddha Book Two

record all of my experiences, how I felt, that was challenging to me and what was rewarding. She said that if I did this, patterns would appear that would change my life."

I was enthralled with her spirit sister and all she'd told Janine and I was curious how much shifting of awareness it created in her.

"has it changes your life?", I asked.

"Immeasurably," she responded.

Janine stood up and walked over to the bookshelf and took down a beautifully decorated notebook. She came over and handed it to me. On the cover were the words, "Celebration journal'. This was the journal Claire had told me about, but I never expected I'd get a chance to see it. I looked up at her and asked whether it was okay for me to open and read it.

She said, "Of course Sam, my life is an open book to you."

I knew that was true and felt so appreciative that I meant so much to her that she would share such personal and profound things with me. That she would share the essence of her life with me. How blessed I felt.

I quickly noted that there were similarities to the entries. They each started out noting a specific event. I'm sure I would have been tempted to 'label' most of the events as 'negative', but she made no mention of that. They were simply statements of fact. Each statement was followed by Janine's 'feelings' about the event and the particulars. Some entries were detailed and others were more general. Some mentioned connections to other people and some were all about her. What I was most taken with were the summaries at the end of each entry. They were always plentiful, and from my reading, they outweighed whatever difficulties were created by the experience.

"This is amazing," I told her. "How has writing in your 'Celebration Journal' shifted things for you?"

"Sam, I now understand that everything I experience in my life is meaningful and connected and exists to serve my greatest good."

Little Buddha Book Two

I'm sure she believed this, but it was certainly beyond my comprehension. I'd read her entries and she'd experienced some very challenging events in her life. There were many things I could not have found valuable or worthwhile and I could not imagine having the patience to remain watchful and alert, while waiting for the benefits to arrive.

"How are you able to be so patient to hear the full message of your experience?", I asked, wanting desperately to know her answer.

"It's because of the power of the vision quest and the divine sense of love I felt from Lia. I know in my heart she spoke the absolute truth. The more time I've spent with her, the deeper the love becomes, so that now, I rarely have any doubts. And by maintaining my 'Celebration Journal' practice, it reinforces the truth."

Schrodinger came thumping into the backyard again. Janine looked out at her and said, "Sam, do you remember this afternoon when Schrodinger was stalking and pouncing on the sun spots on the carpet?"

"Sure, that was pretty funny."

Little Buddha Book Two

"Well we humans are tempted to do the same thing. We think that what we see, our experiences are real, like the sun spots on the carpet are to the cat. We pounce on them, scratch them, try to pick them up or sweep them away, never realizing they are a part of the grand illusion of this life. They are not real but appear real to us."

I felt we'd just changed directions in midstream. She'd been telling me about Lia, her spirit guide and how much she loved her and was loved by her. She told me how she waited patiently now for the intended messages wrapped up inside her experiences. She told me that each and every one existed to serve her greatest good. So where was she going with the whole idea of this life being a part of some grand illusion? I didn't see the connection.

"What are you saying?", I asked.

"I'm saying that every experience points our way to the truth but is not the truth itself. I'm saying that the essence of every experience is a 'spark', a spark which can ignite an awareness of the truth."

Little Buddha Book Two

"Okay, I hear what you're saying, but I don't understand it. What 'truth' are you talking about?"

"The truth is Sam, each of us chose to come here, to this earth plane, to create and experience whatever we desire. Our choices are limitless and there are no restrictions. We can experience tremendous 'highs' and sometimes terrifying 'lows'. We can live here as though it is 'heaven' or as if it is 'hell'. Every one of our choices creates our own personal experience, our path. We can choose 'wisely' or 'foolishly'. We can connect with others or separate ourselves in isolation."

I nodded to her so she would know I was listening, but I didn't want to interrupt her yet. I wanted to hear everything she had to say.

She continued, "Sam, before you arrived here on this earth plane, you knew everything there was to know. At some point however, the essence that is you, made a choice to awaken here on earth. The spiritual part of you, which is always connected to heaven, understood that earth was a place for you to exercise your free will. A place to create and explore. A place with an almost unending spectrum of choices available to you. The spiritual part of

Little Buddha Book Two

you also understood and recognized that earth was a grand illusion, designed for you to experience anything you wished, yet always knowing it was not the real truth."

I couldn't help it. I said, "Claire has told me this same thing and I have just as hard a time hearing you say it. How could my whole existence here not be real? If that's true, then what am I doing here?"

"That is a wonderful question Sam. Do you see how your question is a 'spark', because it ignites in you a desire to know? A desire to remember the truth."

"Wait, I'm still confused. You're saying that my question is a 'spark', because it ignites my desire to know, to remember the truth?" I knew I was repeating her statement, but I had to make sure I heard her correctly.

"Yes," she said.

"So the truth is that I chose to leave 'heaven', which is real, to come to 'earth', which is not real, so that I could create and experience life here, and then if I made certain choices I would 'remember' and 'wake up' to the truth. That I would 'remember' what I'd chosen to

Little Buddha Book Two

'forget'. If all of that is true, what would happen then? Would I cease to exist here on earth? Would I simply evaporate or vanish into thin air?"

I was feeling very lost. Most of what Janine was telling me, Claire had already told me, but this time it struck me so differently. It was completely disorienting, I felt like all of the things in my life that I'd been able to hold on to were now out of reach. I'm sure Janine could sense this because she came over to me and hugged me. I held on tightly. So tightly. She was rocking my world and I needed her to hold still.

I could feel her breathing and I tried to calm down and follow her rhythm. It took quite a while, but finally I stopped shaking. My body began to relax and my breathing eased, until I was somewhat at peace.

Her hug was gentle. It felt real to me. It didn't feel like an illusion. It felt divine.

"What's happening Janine? I don't get it. I don't get any of it. Can you help me, please?"

Little Buddha Book Two

"Sam, I sense your confusion. I've experienced the same thing. It's going to be okay, I promise."

I wanted to believe her, but I needed some more reassurance. I needed to understand. I needed to move beyond my present understanding. I wasn't sure I had that kind of courage or that kind of trust. This whole conversation truly scared me. Some part of me wondered why. Why should this trouble me so much?"

"Janine, what am I so afraid of? Do you know?"

"I do Sam. Before my vision quest this concept was not something I could even consider. It was too big, too challenging, too threatening. There was no way for me to be open to it and no one to guide me. So, I lived as I always had, feeling as though I only knew a small part of the truth. And then my father, Bright Sky, told me there was a way for me, to know a path that led to wherever I dreamed of going. He told me my spirit guide would meet me, sit with me, guide me, love me. If I could summon my courage, he could take the first step with me and prepare my way. I said, "Yes, please my father, do this for me." I can tell you more

Little Buddha Book Two

about this later but what's important right now is that Lia entered my life and poured her love over me and into me. She helped me to see clearly. She still does. She is with me in every moment."

"Sam, I know you think that discovering the truth 'ends' your life. What I'm telling you is that it 'begins' your life. What you feel right now is a host of 'fears'. Fears that your life will spin out of control. And that is true. You will lose 'control'. But the truth is, you aren't in 'control', not the way you've been taught to regard 'control'. Your belief that you can control everything in your life is a big part of the illusion. It is the source in you of many fears. You struggle to exert your desires, not only within yourself, but outside of yourself. There is nothing 'wrong' with this, but if you desire a happy life, you make it all but impossible."

She looked carefully at me to make sure I was paying close attention. I was. It felt like my life depended on it.

"Sam, every one of your fears serve you. This may surprise you. You may feel as others do, that fear is the enemy. That it is to be battled and overcome. Or run away from. Perhaps you

Little Buddha Book Two

know this already, but neither of these choices will bring about peace for you. If you shift your attention, you will see that each fear serves as a 'spark', because it flares up and creates light to see the truth. By sitting with your fears and asking them to show you their message, you can use the 'spark' wisely. When you are at peace, you can hear what they have to say. When you are at peace, you can thank them in advance and bless them for sharing their insight with you. It is very important to realize that every fear unerringly points the way to love. This was a large part of my vision quest. I sat with all of my fears. At times they surrounded me, awaiting their turn to speak. When all had spoken, I felt a great and beautiful emptiness. I felt open. I felt liberated. I felt ready to be filled with something new. And Lia came and filled me with love. I can close my eyes and feel the truth of that love."

"Sam, living from this love has created a whole new life for me. I know that her love for me came from 'heaven'. It is 'heaven'. And I am filled to overflowing. Now that I know this love, this truth, I call it my own. I feel it move in and through me. It is my life blood. At first it was her love that filled me, but now it is my own, because I know the truth, I feel the truth, that we are only love. I offer you this gift, this love

Little Buddha Book Two

that rests at our very core. This love that surpasses all ideas of the mind, that creates new life in us and that brings our full memory back to us and awakens us. You are afraid that remembering that you are love, somehow ends your life here on earth. That knowing this might spoil the grand illusion. What I'm saying is that it opens your heart wide so that living here becomes an extension of heaven. That living with overflowing love pouring from your heart, you offer the world what it most needs. You offer divine rays of love that brings light to the darkness. You live here, on earth as you lived in heaven, a source of emanating love. I offer you this gift of love so that you may 'begin' your life anew."

I looked at her with tears streaming down my cheeks and said, "I love you and accept this gift. I see you."

Little Buddha Book Two

seeds

Little Buddha Book Two

I felt strong, perhaps stronger than ever before. No, that wasn't exactly right. It was more definite than that. I KNEW I was stronger. I'd spent the whole year feeling and thinking about my final conversation last summer with Janine. It was so powerful and although I'm sure there was so much more she could tell me, the essence of what she'd said held fast inside of me. To know that I am made wholly of love was so important to me. It changed things in my life, day to day things and I felt a new balance and a great sense of happiness. I couldn't wait to see Claire and Janine again.

On this first day of summer, I was headed down their alleyway, toward their fence gate. The air was incredibly fresh feeling and the sun was gaining power, creating warmth for the day.

I saw something new as I approached the gate. There was a sign there. It read, 'Welcome June and Gus to the worldwide celebration of your life', I think I knew what that meant. I'd been in touch with June off and on over the past eight months. I knew that she and Gus had become very close and I guessed it was probably only a matter of time before they would get married. Well, perhaps

Little Buddha Book Two

this sign was a way of congratulating them. I'd have to ask as soon as I saw Claire or Janine.

A moment later I felt myself stumbling and just caught my balance before crashing down to the ground. Of course, I knew the cause.

"Hey Schrodinger, watch where you're going!" I yelled. She stopped on the path ahead of me, turned to face me and 'meowed'. I wasn't sure if it was an apology or her way of saying, "No, you watch out!" She gave me an appraising stare and pranced away, her tail high in the air. I'm pretty sure now which kind of meow it was.

"Sorry about that," came a voice from behind me, "she's always in a hurry."

I knew that voice. Sure enough, it was Jamie, Claire's homeschool buddy and one of my newest friends.

"Your cat has some annoying habits you know," I said.

"You can that again! You should try sleeping in the same room with her!" Jamie exclaimed. "Ewww, wet face from cat licks!"

Little Buddha Book Two

"I'll pass," I said, and changing subjects added, "It's so nice to see you again, Jam."

"You too Sam." She was smiling and I noticed how lit up she seemed.

"What's going on Jam?", I asked, feeling like I did so often with Claire, like there was some inside joke I was missing.

"I'm just really happy," she answered. "I think I'm going to get to be the flower girl for the first time in my life. It's taken me a long time to find the right bride and groom."

"Is that the way it works?", I asked. "I thought brides and grooms found the flower girl, not the other way around."

"Well, I don't know about the usual way, but it's how it works for me. Trust me, they're going to want me, and I have just the right flowers picked out."

"So, you're a one stop kind of shop huh? They get flowers and a flower girl all in one."

"Yup, that's the way I roll", she said with a grin.

Little Buddha Book Two

"Hey, what are you two talking about out there?" Claire said, approaching us from the other side of the fence.

She opened the gate and ran to hug us and then placed her forehead against each of ours in turn and said, "I see you."

"It's so good to be seen," we responded.

"So, is it true?", I asked, "are June and Gus getting married?"

"Yes, isn't it wonderful! The ceremony is planned for the last day of summer. It's going to be in our backyard and mom is going to officiate."

"That's fantastic," I said.

"You'll never believe where they're going on their honeymoon. Try to guess," Claire teased.

"They're going on a trip around the world," I answered. I was joking because I could only imagine how much that would cost and neither of them had that kind of money.

"How did you know?" Claire said, stunned that I'd guessed correctly.

Little Buddha Book Two

"I'm going to write this down on my calendar," I told Claire and Jamie. "This is the first time EVER that I've surprised Claire. She always seems to know everything about me. Maybe I'll buy a lottery ticket later since I'm feeling so lucky."

"Seriously Sam, how did you know? They just announced it to Mom and me this morning and said we were the first one they'd told." Claire seemed truly curious.

"Perhaps it might have something to do with the sign on your gate," I said, smiling broadly.

Claire turned and noticed the sign. "Oh, Mom must have put that up there. Good pick up Sam, you're really paying attention!"

We all went into their backyard and sat in the comfy patio chairs. Janine came out with a tray holding four large glasses of iced tea. She set the tray down and came over to hug Jamie and me.

"It's so wonderful to see you both," she said, "how has your journey been since I saw you last?"

Little Buddha Book Two

What an interesting choice of words, I thought. How has my journey been? That question was a keeper for me. I suspected I was going to use that a lot from now on.

We talked for a couple of hours, getting reacquainted and sharing some of our life highlights.

Claire turned to me at one point and asked, "Sam, what did you mean when you said you were going to write down on your calendar that you'd surprised me? What calendar are you talking about?"

I was grateful for the opening to share my latest project with them.

"Well after my last conversation with Janine I did a lot of thinking and feeling and inner searching. The idea that I am love, that I came from love, exist here in a state of love and return to love was incredibly powerful for me. It got me thinking about all of my earth experiences and I decided I wanted to celebrate my life, so I began to create an outline. As I thought more about it, it changed shape and eventually I settled on seven ideas. Seven seemed like the perfect number to me,

Little Buddha Book Two

since there are seven days in a week and this is my CALENDAR project."

They were all looking directly at me. Even Schrodinger was sitting quietly. Her eyes were glued to me and there was only an occasional twitch of her tail.

"Go on Sam," Claire encouraged.

"Well, the categories all mean something different to me, but they're all really special. At the top of each page there is a place for me to write down about a 'Special Event' in my life, a date or occasion of significance to me. You have to understand that there is a page for every day of the year, and seven entries for each day, so I have three hundred and sixty-five, or in the case of a leap year, three hundred and sixty-six days' worth of entries. For you math whizzes, that two thousand five hundred and sixty-two separate entries. Suffice it to say, it's going to take me a while to put the whole calendar together.

Jamie looked at me with a curious expression, then giggled. "It's a good thing you're so old Sam, because at least you've been around long enough to have had that many experiences."

Little Buddha Book Two

"Thanks, I think," I said, stifling a laugh. "You're quite the comedian, aren't you?"

Everyone joined in the laughter and when it died down, Janine asked, "What are the other categories?"

"I'll give them all to you at once, but if you want to ask me some questions, you can. There's an 'Affirmation', which is a positive statement I can tell myself. It's got to be one I really believe in though, not someone else's affirmation that just sounds good. I've found those don't end up meaning very much to me."

"Next, there is a 'Memory' from my life, something that makes me happy, something about a person or a place or accomplishment or experience. Something that lights me up."

"And then there's a 'Gratitude' category. Something I am personally grateful for in my life. It can be small, medium or large. This was one of the easiest to fill in because for quite a while now I've been starting off my daily Feelings Journal listing three things I'm grateful for."

Little Buddha Book Two

"Following that, there are 'Spiritual Journey' entries, which are slices of my spiritual life, like all the 'dots' that connect to make it meaningful."

"Next is 'Good Stuff', which varies a great deal. It can be a saying I like, a poem of mine or someone else's, a song, a story a book I've read or a favorite movie or TV show."

"My last category is 'People', where I write down a person I want to celebrate, someone who had been really influential in my life or someone I deeply love." I looked at each of their faces. They were smiling at me and nodding.

"Awesome idea," Claire said, "well done, grasshopper!"

"I feel like I've just snatched the pebble from your hand Master," I responded.

"What are you two talking about?" Jamie asked.

I turned mental pages in my calendar project and said to her, "October 30, 'Good Stuff' entry: Kung Fu, the TV series", by way of explanation. "It's one of my all-time favorite TV

Little Buddha Book Two

shows Jamie. I have it on DVD, so we'll have to watch it together sometime."

"I'd like that Sam", she said, "I'm into old school TV shows."

"Oh, I almost forgot. In the back of each binder, that houses a month of entries, there is a section of sheet protectors that cover all sorts of miscellaneous things. There are lots of photograph, cards, pictures and memorabilia, like ticket stubs, programs from events and drawings. Mostly, the items are from the month that matches the days entries, but not always. I love the whole project and it's an incredible amount of fun to relive my life, one special day at a time."

Janine asked, "Do you have it here with you?"

"Yes, it's at my cottage. As you can imagine, I'm still in the process of assembling it. I think it might take me more than a year to complete, maybe more. And of course, I'm going to want to add new stuff to it all the time."

"I would love to look at it, if that would be okay with you," Janine asked.

Little Buddha Book Two

"Of course," I said, "my life is an open book to you."

Janine smiled at me, knowing my reference was to what she'd said to me about her 'Celebration Journal' last summer.

Claire and Jamie said together, "We'd like to see it too."

"I'd be happy to share it with you. After all, you're all a part of it in so many ways."

"Awwww," they purred, "how sweet."

The whole rest of the day just melted away. We drifted from one conversation to the next, so easily, so comfortably. Even Schrodinger was relaxed, cat-napping in Jamie's lap."

Late in the afternoon as I was getting ready to leave. Claire held out her hand to me and asked, "Sam, would you like to do an experiment tomorrow?"

"Sure," I said, "what kind of experiment?"

"The kind with seeds and soil and water," she answered. "It's one Jamie and I came up with recently."

Little Buddha Book Two

"It must be fun if the two of you created it. Sure, I'm in." And with that I hugged them each goodbye, promising to be back early the next morning.

It's the next morning now and the cloud cover is pretty dense, letting only a few stray strands of light through the gaps. Actually, this is one of my favorite skys.

As the dark clouds shifted, a huge hole formed and a brilliant shaft of light streaked toward the surface of the ocean. The shaft seemed alive and so beautiful. It hit the water and lit up the cresting waves. The hole shifted again and the glowing beams moved onto the beach and started coming in my direction. I stood still and waited. I heard some gulls cry in the distance and the clang of a warning buoy out at sea. The air was crisp and ruffled my hair, as it wiped past me. I watched as the glorious rays came to rest over me, surrounding me in their intense light. The sand around me looked like it was on fire. I tipped my head back so I could look directly up toward the opening in the sky and I heard a voice. It was speaking directly to me. It was faint at first and I had to focus all of my attention to hear it, and then it was gone. I wondered had I heard it correctly? Yes, I had. I

Little Buddha Book Two

repeated the words to myself, over and over again, desperately wanting to commit them to memory and keep them close to my heart. The voice had said, "my beloved, oh, my beloved, fear nothing and love everything, as I love you." I was overcome with emotion and dropped to the surface of the beach on my knees. I leaned forward and touched my forehead lightly against the sand and wept. Wept like a newborn baby. My tears were joy and something else. Something much more powerful. I knew I was loved. Wholly and intimately loved. Whatever doubt had once been inside of me, had vanished. I was loved. I rested there and gave thanks for a long, long time. Finally, I had the strength to rise and noticed I was standing in the very spot I had first seen Little Buddha six years ago. Perhaps I shouldn't have been surprised, but I was. I knew without question what to write today on my calendar project as a 'Special Event'.

While I was walking to Claire's cottage I considered telling her and Janine and Jamie about this experience, but somehow it seemed too personal to share so soon. I wanted to savor it all to myself for now. It was like a sacred present I'd been given and I wanted to be the only one to unwrap it. I remember Claire telling me once that every decision is

Little Buddha Book Two

open to us and not to question the choices we make that come from our hearts. I was sure that this was one of those choices.

When I arrived, they were all waiting for me. Starring at me would be a better description.

"What?" I asked, feeling a little self-conscious and confused.

"So much for coming first thing in the morning." Jamie said, shaking her finger at me in mock admonishment, "it's already 9:30am."

"What," I said, "that can't be, I left my cottage at 7:00 this morning." I wondered, had time warped somehow? Had it stood still? Was it true that time is a apart of the grand illusion?

"It doesn't matter Sam, you are always worth the wait," Claire said, beaming at me. "You know we love you and that you are a brilliant ray of sunshine to us, right?"

She knew. Of course, she did. Maybe she heard the voice too. Maybe it spoke to her. Maybe the voice shared its love with everyone, like it did with me. I certainly hoped that was true. I certainly hoped that everyone knew how much they are loved. It hit me right then. That

Little Buddha Book Two

was a part of my 'job'. Not really a 'job', more like a 'mission'. Yes, that was it, it was part of my mission, to show love, to be a source of love, to bring heaven to earth. What an awesome thought, what an awesome 'assignment'.

Claire reached out and took my hand in hers. I felt the wonderful warmth of it. She reached out her other hand to Jamie, who took it, while reaching out for one of Janine's hands. Janine held it and then took mine and completed the circle. I felt an immediate vibration. And the vibration grew and I could feel the pulsing energy running round and round between us. We closed our eyes and somehow quite naturally started humming. It wasn't any tune I'd ever heard before. And then I knew it, it was the hum of love. I hadn't known there was such a thing, but I knew it now.

We each eventually gave a squeeze of our hands and let go. I guess I had another entry for my calendar project.

I looked over at the patio table and noticed twelve empty pots sitting there and asked, "So, tell me about this experiment of ours."

Little Buddha Book Two

Claire looked at Jamie. Somehow, even though she was blind, Jamie knew Claire was looking at her and letting her take the lead to explain. I wondered, could Jamie somehow 'picture' each of us? Could she 'know' how we looked and what actions we were taking?

"Well," Jamie stated, "Claire and I wanted to test a theory we have about the way things grow. So, what we're each going to do is to fill three pots with potting soil, then gently place a seed in the middle of the pot. We're all going to keep the three pots in our bedrooms and we're going to water them according to a specific plan. We're going to label the pots 'A', 'B' and 'C'. We'll water pot 'A' every third day, pot 'B' a little every day and pot 'C' three times a day. We'll do this for the next month and see what happens. Did I forget anything Claire?"

"We did talk about whether we could do other things, like play different music to each of them or put our hands over one but not the others, but I think we decided to keep it simple."

"Yes, that's right," Jamie agreed, "we thought it was best not to confuse things. We could always do another experiment later. So Sam, are you game?"

Little Buddha Book Two

"Sure," I responded, "let's do it."

We each took our three pots and marked the outsides with the letters A, B and C, then filled them with soil, planted our seeds gently into the mix and set them aside.

We spent the rest of the day playing games, eating, talking and as was our habit, taking a wonderful nap. Whoever invented naps, I think was a genius.

As the day ended, I hugged them and carried my little seeds in their pots back to my cottage.

I had to admit, I knew next to nothing about plant care, but it seemed to me our watering routine would not favor each of the seeds. I guess I'd find out as time went along.

I was surprised to find that I really cared about the seeds. Shockingly, I named them, although I didn't tell the others about it. I especially wasn't going to tell Jamie since she already enjoyed making fun of me too much.

Since I love crystals, I named seed 'A', Amethyst, seed 'B', Beryl and seed 'C', Calcite, I decided to write down their watering schedule on a 4x6 index card to make sure the

Little Buddha Book Two

experiment went according to plan. After a week I expected to see three tiny shoots appear, but nothing happened. Another week passed and there in pot 'B', was the tip of a little green shoot, popping out of the soil.

"Welcome to the world Beryl," I said out loud. It made me really happy to see her. I know plants probably aren't male and female, but I decided Beryl was a girl.

Over the next couple of days, I eagerly watched her stretch up toward the sun. I confess it really bothered me that Amethyst and Calcite were still 'sleeping' in their pots. Another week went by and still nothing from either of them. But Beryl was now straight and getting taller every day. What a beautiful plant she was going to make. It was the end of week four and time to compare notes with my friends.

I carefully carried my pots in a box to Claire's cottage. When I got there, there were already nine pots set out on the patio table. Not surprisingly, only three contained vibrant green plants. They were all growing out of pot 'B's. Maybe it's foolish or childish, but I felt very sorry for the seeds in pots 'A' and 'C'. I don't think they ever had a chance.

Little Buddha Book Two

Everyone was there and we greeted each other warmly. It appeared I wasn't the only one who felt badly about the 'no growers'.

Jamie was the first to speak, "I've been feeling for signs of growth all month and only 'Betty' is healthy and alive.

I guess I also wasn't the only one to name my plants.

Claire said, "Jamie, the experiment turned out exactly the same for each of us. I guess it really matters how you water them.

They all turned toward me and Janine asked, "Did you draw any conclusions from this experiment Sam?"

"I was wise to them. I'd been thinking this over the entire month and it felt like the whole experiment was set up to see if I could figure out the true purpose. I'd had many ideas but settled on one and it felt accurate to me. I nodded my head and said, "Yes, I did, transparent ladies. I see your metaphor and raise you one." I knew they'd understand my reference, since one of the games we'd played yesterday was poker.

Little Buddha Book Two

"What do you mean Sam," Jamie said, trying unsuccessfully to keep a straight face.

My first thought was that the 'A' pots represented when we don't pay enough attention to ourselves and starve in the process. Watering every three days isn't enough. For the 'C' pots, it's kind of the opposite, because overwatering is like obsessing about everything in our lives. It turns out it matters a great deal what you place your attention on." I stopped and looked at them. They each had a tiny grin on their faces, I knew it, it was a set up from the start. But now was my chance.

"So, what I want to know from you, is what is the deeper meaning of the experiment?"

They stared at me and Jamie asked, "What do you mean Sam, that was the meaning."

"Well, that might be your meaning, but it's not the only meaning. Maybe you each need to think about this overnight, you know, like 'homework'."

Claire was smiling so broadly. I don't think I'd ever seen her quite so radiant.

Little Buddha Book Two

She said, "And so, the student becomes the master. I accept your challenge to find more meaning and I'll let you know tomorrow."

Janine and Jamie nodded in agreement.

We had another great day, this time spending most of it at the beach swimming and boogie boarding. It turned out Jamie always caught the best waves. I wanted to know her secret, but all she said was, "Watch and find out."

I did watch her. She had an uncanny knack of starting to paddle at just the right time. Super impressive.

The next morning, we gathered again at Claire and Janine's cottage.

"Who wants to go first," I asked.

"I do," Jamie said. "Perhaps our experiment was biased from the beginning because we theorized how it would turn out. Maybe we influenced the outcome based on our intention."

I looked at her and smiled. "That's very nice," I said, "but not what I had in mind."

Little Buddha Book Two

Claire decided to jump in saying, "Maybe it's not about the pot or the soil or the water. Maybe the metaphor is that it's about the seed itself, the seed of our personal life and that regardless of circumstances, some seeds will thrive while others perish."

"Also, most interesting, but not what I had in mind. I guess it's up to you, Janine."

"I think it may be very simple. Once we noticed that only plant 'B' was showing signs of growth, we pored all of our love and attention into it and perhaps gave up hope for the others. This happens all the time in life. It's so easy to love the lovable and ignore the seemingly unlovable."

"Beautiful," I said, "and so true, but also, not what I had in mind."

I looked at each of them. They were all shaking their heads slightly.

I said, "Thank you for 'playing along' with me. I hope you know I treasure each of you and your answers and am grateful you chose to believe there was something deeper here to look for. I want to share with you what I saw and felt come alive during this experiment. Although the 'explanations' you gave are beautiful and meaningful, I'd like to offer you a different one."

They all nodded, smiled and spread their arms wide, as a way of showing they were open to hearing what I had to say.

"What came to me was that despite how we choose to treat others or ourselves, there is always love available to us so that we can heal and feel whole. Whether we are starved or overwhelmed, love is the way for us to thrive. The seeds could not water themselves, to provide this love. They were dependent on their connection to the world and to the source of all water, all love. The seeds could not thrive without others, just as we cannot. We are truly whole when we give love and receive love.

I looked at their faces again. There were tears staining each of their cheeks, but they were smiling.

Claire looked at me and said, "Well this certainly qualifies to be written on my calendar project. Thank you, Sam, my friend and master."

Little Buddha Book Two

change orders

Little Buddha Book Two

It was another beautiful day. The sun was rising higher and playing games with the ocean surface, creating brilliant glistening patterns. The ever-changing sparkles always fascinated me. I know that when the reflections stayed in one place it was too bright to look at, but when they constantly moved and shifted, it was radiant and beautiful to watch. I wondered how, when although it was nearly the same scene, one was painful and the other was pleasurable. And I wondered if this was some sort of metaphor for life. Could I shift my view of anything and alter how it felt to me?

My inner reflections were interrupted by a loud noise and a sensation on my left leg. I looked down and there was Schrodinger. She gazed up at me, meowed again and moved her paw on my leg.

"What do you want?" I asked.

In response, she stretched both paws up my leg and meowed some more. I reached down and picked her up. She moved in my arms so that she was laying on her back, like she was a baby. Her head nuzzled into me and she started purring. Even though I was a dog person, I thought she was a pretty 'cool' cat. She seemed to purr louder in response to my

Little Buddha Book Two

thoughts. I decided to head to Claire's cottage and see if anyone was up.

When I arrived, Janine was just coming out of their alleyway gate. She was carrying a large box and I was immediately curious.

"Hi Janine," I said, "do you need any help?"

I put Schrodinger down so I'd be able to carry the box she held or another one if there were more. Schrodinger meowed in protest.

"Oh, hi Sam," Janine responded, "there's three more boxes on the patio. It would be great if you could get them and meet me at my car, thanks."

I went through their gate and saw the boxes immediately. They were smaller than the one she carried and would be easy to move in one trip. Once I was at her car, I loaded them in her trunk and asked, "Are you going to the Center this morning?"

Janine had begun working at the Center earlier this summer. It was a kind of community gathering place. They ran all sorts of programs and I never knew what they'd be up to next. Janine had told me that she and Claire and

Little Buddha Book Two

Jamie had all decided to do some volunteering. They'd each picked different 'helping' organizations and were having a great time meeting and getting to know folks.

"Yes," Janine responded, "I'm heading out in a few minutes. Do you want to come with me? We're doing a special project and I think you might really enjoy it."

The Center was a place where everyone was welcome. The sign that hung over the door proclaimed, 'All are one. All are welcome. All are loved'. I'd been there several times and the people who came there all knew that the sign was true and they could feel what a special place it was.

"Absolutely," I said. "Do I have time to say hello to Claire?"

"I'm sorry Sam, she's already left to go to the Shelter. They're having an open breakfast this morning and she's helping to serve. She'll be home later, so you can connect when we see her."

"Sounds good to me," I said and asked Janine, "what's in all of the boxes?" I ought to have known better than to ask.

Little Buddha Book Two

"It's a surprise," was her response, which came with a sly sort of smile.

I had begun 'categorizing' Janine and Claire's smiles. They each had a wide variety and it was fun to see if I could tell in advance what each of them meant.

We got in her car and headed off to the Center. When we arrived, there were lots of people present. There was a wide mix of ages, from toddlers to grandparents. Janine had previously told me that it was one of the reasons she was attracted to the Center, because of its diversity.

Several teenagers came over to the car and greeted us. I thought this was really unusual. Most teenagers, in my experience, were pretty standoffish. They seemed to hang back and wait for grown-ups to approach them. But here they were coming right up to us and asking if they could help.

Janine greeted each of them by name and asked them to carry the boxes and put them on one of the tables in the main room.

Little Buddha Book Two

A few moments later a Senior Citizen bus pulled up and quite a few elderly men and women got off. I was surprised to see a swarm of kids immediately surround them. The kids appeared to me to be from six to nine years old. I was close enough to hear them and they were all talking at the same time. It surprised me to hear their conversations. Each elderly person knew each child's name and all of the kids called all of the older folks, Grandma or Grandpa. It appeared they had a very intimate relationship and I found it incredibly touching. I couldn't remember experiencing this before, so I turned to Janine and asked, "Is this new?"

Of course, she knew what I was referring to.

"Yes Sam, isn't it awesome?"

I nodded my agreement and asked, "How did this happen?"

By way of an answer, Janine took hold of my hand and said, "Come with me and see for yourself."

This was the first time she'd held my hand like this. There were other times, but they'd been when she was demonstrating some technique or helping me with an art project. This felt very different. Different and special. It gave me goosebumps and I felt my face flush a little.

Inside the Center it was a beehive of activity, but instead of it feeling frenetic and chaotic, it felt alive and vibrant. There was a kind of buoyant energy and it seemed to me that everyone was so happy to be there.

"Hi Janine," a young woman said enthusiastically. I recognized her. Her name was Beth and she was the director of the Center.

Janine responded with a warm hug and a greeting.

Beth turned toward me and said, "Welcome back Sam, it's so nice to see you again." She looked at Janine and then back to me. She pointed toward Janine and exclaimed to me, "I have to tell you, this woman is amazing. Do you see how much fun everyone is having? It's all because of her. She's a real god send."

I'd never heard truer words. "You're so right," I said.

Janine smiled at Beth and said, "Shall we get this party started?"

Little Buddha Book Two

Beth nodded affirmatively and called out to everyone, "Okay everybody let's all find a seat at one of the tables so Janine can explain this morning's activity."

There was a lot of commotion until finally everyone found a seat. I looked around and many of the 'grandparents' had toddlers in their laps.

Janine stood and faced the group. "This morning we're going to dream while we're awake."

Several of the children began talking with each other and one asked, "How can we do that, I only dream when I'm asleep?"

"Wonderful question Omar, thank you for asking." Janine smiled at him and he looked so proud to have been acknowledged.

Janine said, "Inside these boxes are long strips of cloth with holes at one end. The holes are reinforced with grommets, so they won't tear. There is also a very large fabric wall hanging with an outline of a tree on it. And all over the tree there are hooks sewn into the fabric so that the cloth strips can hang on

Little Buddha Book Two

them." As she was speaking she took the materials out of the boxes. When she unfurled the fabric wall hanging with the tree outline, there were lots of 'oohs' and 'ahhs' from the kids.

It was so much fun to see their eyes light up. I thought I could even sense their imaginations come alive.

Janine continued, "This is a project you can do by yourself or with someone else. What I'm suggesting is that you each take a piece of paper and pencil, then sit quietly and close your eyes. As you become peaceful, imagine within yourself what your special dreams are for your life. Let them all flow into your awareness. Then, when you've collected them all, open your eyes and write them down on your piece of paper. Does anyone have any questions?"

A small boy raised his hand and Janine smiled and said, "Good morning Maleek, what would you like to know?"

He jumped to his feet and with a toothy grin, he asked, "Can I write down ALL of them or is there a limit?"

Little Buddha Book Two

Janine responded, "There are no limits here or in your life. You can do or be anything you desire, so please feel free to write down everything you dream. This is true for each of you, without exception."

It appeared to me that everyone was anxious to get started, but Janine had some further instructions.

"Once you are happy with your dream list, help yourself to as many cloth strips as you'd like and begin to decorate them and bring them to life." She pointed to all of the supplies they could possibly want in order to create their dream strips. "After you're finished, please feel free to hang up your strips on the dream tree. If you need any help or want to ask me anything, just give me a shout."

A moment later it was a controlled pandemonium of activity. Some folks worked by themselves, but most worked together. I couldn't discern any pattern because people of all ages mixed freely and easily. They seemed to change partners and everyone made sure that all of the youngest and oldest had the help they needed. It fascinated me. I'd never seen such a wide range of ages working together like this.

Little Buddha Book Two

As time passed, people began approaching the fabric dream tree wall hanging. They'd stare at it trying to decide exactly where they wanted their "dreams" to be placed. It was great fun to watch, but I also had my own dream strips to create. One idea kept popping up so I wrote it down. It surprised me because it was so much more powerful than my other ideas. What I'd written was, 'vision quest' and I'd decorated it with dazzling gold glitter. I wondered if it would come true. I wondered if any of the dreams on the tree would come true. What did it take to make dreams turn into reality?

As I was thinking this, Janine began speaking again.

"You are such a special group and I want to honor our time together and not rush anyone, so please know that if you're not done with this project, I'll be leaving the dream tree here. This means you can add your dream strips any time you want. It's important for you to know that you have forever to dream." Janine was quiet a moment, as if she was letting that sink in. "In a minute we're going to do the second half of our morning project."

Little Buddha Book Two

About ten minutes later it had calmed down a bit. There were refreshments on several long tables, so I helped myself and brought over some juice and a cookie to Janine. She smiled brightly and asked a favor of me.

"Sam, would you hand out a notebook and a pen to everyone and take one for yourself?"

"Sure," I responded, and went about my task.

"Okay, bright lights," she said looking at each face, "Sam has passed out a notebook and pen to each of you. I'm going to ask you to write the words, 'Gratitude Journal' on the cover of your notebook."

Again, there was a lot of commotion as everyone did as she asked. Several of the children needed assistance and a few of the grandparents did as well. What I saw astounded me. The group of teenagers who had approached us when we arrived were circulating and making sure everyone got the help they needed. Simply amazing.

Janine waited until it seemed quieter and continued with her 'suggestions', since she didn't believe in strong direction.

Little Buddha Book Two

"On the inside of your notebooks I'm going to ask you to write down what you are grateful for in your life. Although you're starting this today, I'm recommending you write in your journal every day. Write the small stuff and the big things and everything in between. Write anything that comes into your mind, anything that your heart and spirit say to you. I want you to know that gratitude inspires your dreams. It gives them energy to become real in your life. Gratitude exceeds all limits and opens your heart wide. It restores your balance and lifts you up. I start every day by writing down three things I am grateful for. Sometimes I get on a roll and write a lot more. I write whatever my heart speaks to me. I trust my heart and my spirit to create my most meaningful life here. You can trust yours too. So, take a moment or two or more and jot down a few things you are grateful for."

There was instant activity. Notebooks were opened and pens flew across pages. There was laughter and hugging. It was infectious and delightful. I was so happy that she'd invited me this morning and that I'd accepted her invitation.

Little Buddha Book Two

"Next time we're going to talk more about your dreams and how they come true in your life. We're going to give them power and then watch them catch fire and come alive."

I could feel the excitement in the air and see it on their faces. They believed Janine. Whatever doubts about their dreams they may have had before, they seemed inspired and hopeful now. There was a feeling I sensed that anything was possible, that everything was possible.

Janine spoke again. "I want you all to know that each of you is connected to the source of love and you are connected to one another. Each of you can change anything in your life. I want you to know that all changes come from your sense of love and gratitude and rise higher and higher through the inspiration of your dreams. It is the way of all change. First, emerging from the inside, then taking flight into the world. You are each connected to the one source that is the fountain of all love and this love inspires all life."

There was rapt attention to her every word. I found myself mesmerized and inspired. She was so gifted, such an incredible bright light. I felt so profoundly fortunate that she was in the

Little Buddha Book Two

center of my life. I believe, in that moment, I felt a new dream arise in me. It's one I'd seen coming, but only in tiny glimpses. Now I saw it fully and it took my breath away. I knew what I wanted most in my life. Her. I wanted to be with Janine. I wondered again about her taking my hand in hers as we entered the Center this morning. Did it mean something or was she just pulling me along with her? Did she feel something for me too? Surprisingly, these questions led me to another. Was I 'available'? Was I ready for a relationship? I knew I still had a lot of what many people called 'baggage'. I wanted to be free and clear. I wanted my heart to be wide open. I wanted to feel clean and fresh and ready. How was that ever going to happen? And then it came to me. I looked down at my cloth strip. I looked at the beautiful gold glittered letters spelling out 'vision quest' and I had my answer. I stood up and went over to the fabric dream tree, I reached up and placed a hook on one of the high limbs and said a prayer to myself, 'I dream of the truth of this dream, may it be so'.

I turned and headed back to my seat. As I did, I saw Janine look at me. It was a whole new smile, one I'd never seen before and I felt completely alive and grateful. What a fabulous morning.

Little Buddha Book Two

Sign language

Little Buddha Book Two

Sign language

There's only a few weeks left in the summer and it feels bittersweet to me. We have June and Gus's wedding to look forward to, but then I have to leave for home and work. I wonder what it will be like one day when I retire and am able to stay here if I want to. There is a tremendous pull on me to stay in Claire and Janine's orbit. But of course, Claire and Jamie will continue to grow and eventually move on with their lives. Maybe they'll go away to college or more likely, join the Peace Corp or volunteer somewhere out there in the wide world. Somewhere that needs them. Needs their unique gifts and heart of love. I wonder about Janine. What will she do when Claire leaves. Will there be anything to hold her here? I wonder, if I came to live here, would I be enough to keep her here? She's been on my mind a lot lately and some intriguing things have happened recently that make me think I may mean more to her than I'd previously thought. I want to ask Claire about it, but I decide that's not fair to either of them. If I want to know what Janine is thinking, I would benefit from asking her. This would be quite a departure from my normal way of handling things. I've been a "beat around the bush" kind of guy my whole life. Maybe I've had a few too

Little Buddha Book Two

many rejections, so I don't want to approach things directly, even though I know it's the best way. It's not like I'm the only one who does this, but there's no comfort in that kind of company.

This all makes me think of a conversation I had with Claire a week or so ago. We were talking about sign language. She'd taken several classes because there were some kids at the Shelter who were hearing impaired and only one person could 'talk' with them. She wanted the kids to know that she cared about them, so she learned and practiced with them every time she saw them. They responded to her and brightened noticeably in her presence. I had gone with her numerous times and it always inspired and amazed me to see how quickly she connected with them. It was so beautiful to watch.

Our conversation centered around a different kind of sign language though. At first, I didn't understand what she was talking about. Nothing new there since I rarely understood her stories, until she gave me some examples.

"Sam", she said, "watch their eyes. I know it's interesting for you to see the 'conversation' of

Little Buddha Book Two

our hands, but our eyes tell the more significant story."

I didn't know what Claire meant, but I did as she asked. I had to move around a bit so I could look more directly at them and see their faces, especially their eyes. There was a great deal of shifting in their gazes. At times their eyes might sparkle and then, depending on what they were 'talking about', they might go hard or vacant or look away altogether. Each shift of focus and attention was a sign. Claire knew how to reach them. She knew a deeper truth to their stories, one I would have completely missed, had she not told me where to look. Claire astounded me with her wisdom. And it was important to me to know her wisdom came from her kindness, her generosity and her love.

At times, there were some challenging kids at the shelter, what some might call 'hard cases'. I was afraid of them, even the ones who were physically smaller than me. I knew they didn't pose any real threat to me, but even so, I was truly afraid of them. When they came into the room, I always found somewhere else to be. But not Claire. She was fearless.

Little Buddha Book Two

I asked her once, "How can you be so at ease around them?"

Her answer was simple and direct.

"Sam, there is no 'them', there's only 'us'."

"I don't understand. I mean, I do, in theory, but I guess I don't in practice. What do you see? What are the 'signs' you see?"

She looked over at Graham, one of the most challenging kids and said, "You are looking on the outside. You don't understand their life and a part of you 'fills in the blanks' and decides who they are based on their appearance. That's really the same thing as 'labeling' your experiences before you've had a chance to receive their message."

I asked her, "So what do you see when you look at them?"

She smiled. It was one of her most delightful smiles. She looked at me and said. "Sam, as I shift my gaze toward Graham, I see his whole being radiate an intense reddish light. It is a defensive projection meant to warn others to stay back or stay away. He's radiating all of his fears outward into the world. They are too

Little Buddha Book Two

intense for him to hold them inside. I know they are not who he is, nor who he wants to be, so I look past them. I look deeply into him until I see his shimmering beautiful heart. I see to his core, where he is love, just as I am love. I am not prevented from seeing his true self because of the boisterous, blustery, angry front he shows to the world. My heart calls out to his heart and his heart answers. I know he is made of love and he sees me for who I am and responds to me through the tiniest cracks. For him it's a twitch at the corner of his mouth. That's his 'sign'. His sign that the door is open and I can approach. And if he sees that I can read the other signs he gives, he will let me in."

"You are so brave," I tell her. "He scares me. I don't know what he's capable of and he could really hurt me. He could hurt you."

Claire nodded her head. "I understand Sam, but do you realize that he's reading your 'signs', your small gestures and the look on your face? He senses how you feel and knows you don't trust him. The only response he feels he can give to you is to push you away. He does this before you push him away. He's been hurt so much and so often that this is how he survives."

Little Buddha Book Two

I stared at her and said," But, he accepts you because he sees the signs you're giving him, that you know who he is, that you know he's made of love, the same as you?" It was both a statement and a question.

"Yes, and the twitch is my opening. It's his sign that I can continue. That he'll see if I am for real. The moment he senses that I am not genuine, he'll close down and force me out."

"What a hard way to live," I said. "Is there any way he can be healed?"

"Healing is always a choice," Claire responded.

I heard her words but I didn't understand their meaning. Was she really saying that it's a choice to heal? That would seem to make it pretty simple. We'd just focus on some part of us that didn't feel 'well' or 'whole' and 'decide'. We'd 'choose' to be healed. I was confused, as usual. How could it be that simple? After all there were some pretty serious conditions and diseases out there. What Claire was saying seemed too simple and far too incredible to believe.

Little Buddha Book Two

"Can you explain what you mean please?", I asked.

Claire placed one of her hands on my heart and the other on the top of my head, what she called my crown. She asked me to close my eyes and breathe in and out slowly. I could feel myself instantly relax. She held these positions for a couple of minutes then released her hands. She asked me to open my eyes and sit with her. I felt so grounded and at ease. I knew this was her way of helping me center, so I could truly hear and understand her.

"Sam, do you remember me telling you that when you decided to come to earth there was a part of you that would always be connected to heaven?"

"Sure. You said that I chose to forget most or all of what I knew in heaven, so that I could experience and create my earth life. And you told me that the part of me that was connected to heaven was my spirit. You said that my spirit was always connected to the divine, the one essence, to the source of love."

"Yes, well there's more to it that I'd like to share with you now. Your body has both physical DNA and what I call spiritual DNA. It's

Little Buddha Book Two

like a blueprint for your spiritual experiences here on earth. None of these experiences are cast in stone. You have free will and you can always choose your path. Most of the time you are not aware of your spiritual plan, but you are still living according to it. Inside your spiritual DNA there is an inherent ability to heal any condition or disease you experience."

"Wait," I said, "did I just hear you correctly? Did you say we can heal anything?"

"Yes, that's what I know to be the truth."

"If that's true then why don't we? It's crazy to think that we'd choose to continue experiencing some awful disease, if we knew that we could heal it. I mean, what would be the point?"

"Sam, I understand your confusion. Let me share some more and you can ask me that question again if you're still uncertain."

I nodded for her to continue, but I'm not sure my mind was open enough to hear her. I would try though. I always tried for her.

"The healing process is all about moving from fear to love. It's important to know what each

Little Buddha Book Two

fears message is for us. It's important that we ask ourselves, what am I to know that this experience is here to show me. And then it becomes important to listen and then move into faith, because what you believe is what you experience.

I must still have looked confused, so Claire continued.

"Sam, although it our nature to want immediate results, it can take time to fully receive some messages. Sometimes we don't experience healing when we most desire it. Sometimes we give up hope that healing is even possible. Sometimes the message is so deeply buried within us that our patience is exhausted while trying to discover it. Part of the healing process is learning patience and trust. Trust that inside the message there are the seeds and the fruit of equal or greater value for that which is currently unhealed."

I'm afraid I'm not a very good student at times because this was too broad a statement for me. I liked practical answers, not theoretical ones. So, I gave her a sign.

Apparently, she noticed, because she winked at me and continued her explanation.

Little Buddha Book Two

"Sam, no matter what the diagnosis is, the truth is that you have the power to heal and move into wholeness. From a certain point of view, all disease is a misperceiving of an experience we've encountered, without the awareness of its truth."

I shook my head.

"I'm sorry Claire but you're actually making it worse, not better. Maybe it's just my opinion, but disease is far to prevalent to be written off as easily as you're suggesting."

"Sam, I'm not saying that disease doesn't 'appear' real to us, nor that we don't experience it as if it is real. But I am saying it isn't the whole truth. It is the expression of our fears. And these fears generate tangible physical, emotional, mental and spiritual outcomes. As I've said before, fear plays a very important role in our lives because it always points the way toward love. And love is always the answer. If we truly sit with our fears and the conditions it creates, and if we listen fully and carefully, we can hear the message or messages being sent through us. And if we send love to each of our fears, they release and disappear. As this happens you are able to heal anything.

Little Buddha Book Two

"I think I need some processing time," I told her. "What it feels like to me is that your statement is a set up for more challenges because if you don't heal, you might feel twice the victim. The first time because your fear created it and the second time because you couldn't receive the message or send it enough love to heal it."

I truly appreciate that you're listening so carefully Sam. Let me see if I can be clearer. Let's take Graham as an example. Would you agree that he is a very troubled teenager?"

"Yes, definitely," I said.

"Well, imagine if he lets me into his world and feels comfortable enough to express his fears. And then, in the sharing process, he feels my love for him. Imagine this inspires him to talk about his fears to the point where he is able to find the value in them. Imagine that once he sees this value, he can express love to it, to thank it for its message and then release the fear and keep the message. Can you imagine the impact this would have on him?"

"So, you're saying that his condition, his troubled soul, exits because of his fears and

Little Buddha Book Two

that once these fears are recognized, and their message or messages are received, that he can show them love and let them go and in this process be healed?"

"Yes, exactly. Sometimes we're able to work through this process by ourselves and then there are times when we need the help and support and love of others."

"Okay, I'm starting to understand this. Keep going please."

"Do you remember when I was eight and had cancer?", Claire asked.

"Of course. I felt so helpless and afraid for you. I remember you said Michael had a different approach to healing than your doctor, who had told you to 'fight and never give up and never give in'. You told me that Michael said that 'fighting' was feeding your condition more fear and that that always created conflict. I remember you said that Michael told you love was the key and he worked with you to help you see how your life was about connecting the dots with love."

"Very good Sam, you have an excellent memory," Claire responded. "While I was

Little Buddha Book Two

receiving the medical treatments, I found that my body needed a period of time of inactivity. I found that slowing down and going inward and connecting with my spiritual self, opened my whole world up. I sat and listened, and in the silence, I discovered so many truths which were previously hidden to me. If I had not experienced that disease, I don't believe I would have found all these treasures. Although I didn't recognize all of the fears under the surface of my life, they were there. Michael knew this and patiently and lovingly helped me explore and find them. And he sat with me. He didn't talk about them, because it was my journey, but he did sit with me and keep me company. And I knew he loved me and that helped me to move into my own truth. I found that whatever the hardships I created through my fears, I discovered a beauty far beyond them. I discovered the open space created by the release of these fears. And I discovered that love came and filled the open space then overflowed from me. It's this love that I connect with when I'm with others. I know the truth that everyone here is from love and that being reminded of this is a wonderful gift I can give them. And with this gift they can remember who they are and know the source of all healing."

Little Buddha Book Two

She stopped for a moment and took a deep breath.

"You see Sam, we are all a source of love. We are each a conduit to the one divine ocean of love. We are each capable of healing, no matter what the cause. In a very real way our fears created our disease or condition and our discovery of the message or messages they came to share with us is the key to healing. Each message provides 'signs' for us to see. Listening to these messages, sitting with them, accepting them, loving and thanking them, creates an awesome inner awareness. And this leads to our ability to release each fear. Love is always the answer. And when we have truly seen and felt our fears and shown them all our overwhelming love, we are healed."

"Breathtaking," I said, "simply breathtaking. I understand what you're telling me. I really get it now and thank you so much. I am so extremely glad that you are my friend."

I felt my heart melt in her presence and I bowed slightly toward her, to honor her. I believed she'd know what that 'sign' meant.

"I love you too, Sam," she said.

Little Buddha Book Two

New beginnings

Little Buddha Book Two

The excitement was starting to build. June had been here for about a week and she and Gus had been very busy consulting with Janine, Claire and Jamie about their wedding plans. They were all sitting around the dining room table at the moment, going over a few last-minute details. The idea was that all of the arrangements would be set a couple of days before the ceremony, so that everyone could relax and enjoy themselves.

Somehow, I knew it would not be a conventional wedding. It didn't seem that that would suit any of them. I was trying to stay out of the planning process and hang around, mostly to be a 'gopher'. You know, 'go for this' and 'go for that'. I recognized the value of keeping my ideas to myself, since there were already a lot of 'cooks in the kitchen'.

While everyone else was preoccupied with the wedding arrangements, I was making some plans of my own. I'd called Michael and asked if I could come out west to visit him. He of course said 'yes' and was delighted that we'd have a chance to get to know each other better. He'd asked me if there were something in particular that I wanted to do or some places I wanted to visit, Clearly, he'd guessed or knew my motivation. I'd been thinking about it

Little Buddha Book Two

all summer and now it was time to commit to a firm decision.

'Michael," I'd said on our last phone call, "I want to go on a vision quest," and then I'd asked him if he would be my guide. He seemed genuinely honored to be asked, but there was hesitation in his voice as he answered.

"Sam, I'm so glad you've decided to seek your spirit guide, but I am not the one you need. It would be best if you asked Bright Sky, He's helped many on their journeys and there are things he can teach you that I cannot. I will be here to help you in the background, but trust me, you want Grandfather as your guide."

I conceded that Michael would know better what would be best for me, but I'd never met Bright Sky and I was feeling a bit intimidated, since I'd hear so much about him. I knew how important he was to Claire and Janine and the fact that he was Janine's father heightened both my curiosity and my anxiety. In my weak moments I wondered, what if he doesn't like me? Or what if he thinks I am not worthy of his time?

Little Buddha Book Two

My conversation with Michael ended up with me promising to call Bright Sky soon to ask for his help. Before Michael hung up, he told me to relax and that Bright Sky would welcome me with open arms. I wanted to believe him. I felt like I had a lot invested in Bright Sky's reaction to me.

Thinking about this reminded me about Claire's homecoming. I remember Janine saying Claire had been out west visiting her father and grandfather, I knew her grandfather was Bright Sky, but we'd never spoken about her father. I wondered all sorts of things. Why wasn't he here living with her and with Janine? It made me really uncomfortable thinking about him. Lately Janine seemed to be showing more interest in me and her interest felt very personal. We'd spent more time together than ever before and I really liked it. I wondered if Claire's father and Janine were divorced. I desperately needed to find out what was going on.

The wedding party planners were getting up from the table and Claire was headed in my direction.

I called to her. "Hey, Sunshine, can I talk with you for a minute?"

Little Buddha Book Two

She was grinning as she approached. Did that mean that she already knew what I wanted? Probably. You'd think that might make this easier, but it didn't. I was feeling hesitant and started to second guess myself.

'Sam, while we were all talking about June and Gus's wedding, it came up about the day my mom and dad got married. Did you know his name was John?"

She'd just said 'was' in reference to her father, so I blurted out, "What do you mean 'was' John?"

Claire smiled. I think she already knew about my concerns, so she made it easy for me to ask about her father. She was such a kind and thoughtful person.

"I said 'was' because he died when I was very young. I can only remember what he felt like and how he smelled. He always wore Old Spice after shave. I can smell it every time I close my eyes when I want to remember him. I wish I knew more, but's all I have, except for my spiritual connection to him. I don't really mean 'except', like that's a little thing, because it's not. It's a very big thing. We 'talk' all of the time."

She stopped for a moment and looked at me, then continued, "He was a firefighter and he'd been inside a house when the roof collapsed. The other firefighters tried to get to him but they couldn't because the heat was too intense. It was really hard on them and they all cried at his funeral. Mom tried to console them, but that only seemed to make it worse. I guess they blamed themselves. It's so hard sometimes to accept mercy and forgiveness and love from others when you can't give it to yourself."

"I'm so sorry Claire. It must have been hard growing up without a dad."

Claire shrugged her shoulders and said, "Actually Sam, it was just always my mom and me. I didn't miss what I didn't know and my mom is so terrific and was always there for me. She's the most wonderful person I know."

Well, that answered one question but brought up another. I hesitated asking but she smiled and nodded and I took that to be her permission.

Little Buddha Book Two

"Before you arrived home your mom told me you were out west visiting your father and grandfather, I don't understand, what did she mean?"

"Well you know I spent time with Bright Sky, but we've never talked about my visit with my father."

"Sam, I spent a great deal of time with my spirit father. I call him, Abba. During my vision quest he came to me and he's never left. He's still with me, guiding me, reassuring me, loving me. He is there for me in every way I could ever want or need. I asked him to come and he came. You don't know this yet, but I'd been on a vision quest the year before too. I got back before you arrived for the summer, so you never missed me. On that vision quest my spirit mother came to me. She is so beautiful, so wonderful. I asked her to come be with me and she came. Her name is Na'a. She lives inside of me, in the deepest, most sacred place. I don't ordinarily talk about father and mother spirit and my connections to them, but it's important that you know now."

Why was it important now, I wondered? Why in this moment?

Little Buddha Book Two

She'd kept both of these experiences to herself all this time. I didn't understand. I guess it showed on my face. It felt like she was keeping something important from me. I knew I was taking this personally and that rarely, if ever, served me, but somehow, I couldn't help it.

She looked sad for a moment and then brightened and regained her loving gaze.

"Sam, both experiences are very deeply personal to me. I'm not ready to share them with anyone yet. One day I know I will be, but not right now. I want to treasure them in my own heart. Please try to understand."

I nodded to her. "I don't believe I could ever be unhappy with you Claire. You mean the world to me and I can certainly wait until you are ready to share."

"Thank you, Sam. It's also important that you know that there are things that each of us need to hold inside ourselves to allow them time to sink into place, to shift and fill our hearts to full and overflowing."

She tipped her head a little and looked out of the corner of her eyes at me.

Little Buddha Book Two

"You'll understand better when I see you next summer, after you've had your own vision quest."

Of course, she knew. Maybe Michael had told her or even Bright Sky.

"No Sam, no one told me, but I see it in your eyes and I feel it in your heart. You are ready and so you will go and you will also find. You will find all of your missing pieces and you will return, whole and complete."

I felt the prophecy in her words. It gave me an enormous sense of peace. I asked her, "Does your mom know too?"

"Yes, silly, of course she knows. She is very happy for you. And so am I."

Later that day we all gathered for dinner. June and Gus both told us about parts of their honeymoon trip around the world that they were looking forward to.

June said, "The part I'm most happy about is visiting Peru." She went on to say, "You all may not know this but I've sponsored a series of children there my whole life. One of them,

Little Buddha Book Two

Maria, worked especially hard and became very successful in business. She's the one who is paying for our honeymoon. She said that if it weren't for me and for my sponsorship, she would never have survived and it is her great pleasure to "sponsor" me now. We've never met in person and I'm so looking forward to meeting her and her family."

"That's fabulous," I told June, "what a remarkable story." I turned toward Gus and asked, "And how about you Gus, where are you most looking forward to visiting?"

He grinned and said, "I guess that would have to be Greenland."

That certainly sparked my interest. I wondered why of all the places in the whole world he'd pick some remote location like Greenland. I didn't get the chance to ask because Jamie piped up first.

"Are you serious or joking around?", she demanded.

"Totally serious," Gus responded, "that's where we first came ashore after that perfect storm I told you about. When our crew set foot on land, we each bowed down and kissed the

Little Buddha Book Two

earth. We made a promise to show our gratitude to the folks that lived there, for all of their kindness and support. I've carved an 'Appreciation' plaque and I want to hand it to them in person along with some money my shipmates and I saved to help fund their children's education. I still have a very deep sense of love and loyalty to those who helped us when we needed it the most. I can't wait to share this with them."

I was feeling a bit teary eyed. I was awestruck by the circle of generosity relayed in these two stories. Did I feel a profound sense of gratitude for anything in my life, like what June and Gus did? Immediately, I knew the answer to that question. YES! I had a profound sense of gratitude for Janine and Claire. I don't know how my life would have turned out if I'd never met them, but I knew it would have likely continued to be shallow and unrewarding. My life now is so full and rich and deep, because of them. My experiences are so intimate and filled with spirit. I knew there was no earthly way to repay them for what I'd received. I also knew they would never have expected it, which made it all the more sweet. I felt such incredible love for both of them. I was so glad I didn't have to travel all the way around the

Little Buddha Book Two

world to tell them. They were both right here. Both in the heart of my life.

I felt four arms surround me. Janine and Claire were standing next to me, hugging me, loving me. I cried openly, not even trying to hold back my tears of joy. How simply marvelous it is to be held in the arms of love.

Well, it's the day of the wedding ceremony and I've just learned it will be held on the beach by candlelight, and by moonlight, if it clears up a bit.

Everyone seems especially happy and lots of guests arrived throughout the day. June's uncle Doug was in a wheelchair and was quite elderly, but he wanted to be here to 'give June away' and to wheel her down the alleyway. Gus had arranged to have plywood sheets laid the entire length of the alleyway and onto the beach so he could roll easily to the ceremony. Maheer said it would be his honor to assist in helping Doug. They'd seemed to form a quick bond, since Doug had spent time in Lebanon during his Merchant Marine travels.

Of course, it was easier for Gus's relatives and friends, since they mostly lived locally. He'd

Little Buddha Book Two

lived here ever since he'd retired from being a fisherman. He'd said this location was a dream come true.

I knew he'd meant it because he'd met Claire and June. What a beautiful series of connecting dots.

As evening approached Janine asked everyone to assemble in the cottage's backyard. The mood was bright and joyful and of course, the decorations were magnificent. The lights Claire and I had woven among the hearts on the fence were spectacular.

Everyone quieted into silence. And then there was a loud 'thump'. I guess Schrodinger didn't want to miss the big event. She'd been tightrope walking along the top of the fence rail and launched herself, landing in front of June and Gus. She came over toward me, so I leaned down to pick her up. I immediately noticed her collar. I'd never seen her wear one, so I was surprised and then shocked because there were two beautiful rings dangling from it.

"What do we have here?" I asked her. She meowed and nuzzled into me, burying her head into my chest. Maybe this was part of the

Little Buddha Book Two

unconventional wedding, having a ring bearing cat. I had seen Gus with the cat earlier, but it seemed crazy to me to trust her to be in the right place at the right time with the rings. I couldn't see myself ever trusting a cat that much.

It took about fifteen minutes, but everyone was assembled on the beach and amazingly the moon had come out from behind a bank of clouds. It was full, had a faint bluish cast to it and was so bright, we could read easily by its light.

Janine stood in front of June and Gus, facing them and the assembled gathering. She was dressed in a long white flowing gown with glowing sequins in the pattern of angel wings. That seemed absolutely perfect to me.

She smiled and nodded to June and Gus and asked them if they were ready to offer their vows to each other.

Earlier in the day I'd discovered that they'd written them together. They'd sat at Gus's house by candlelight and alternated writing sentences until their vows were complete.

Little Buddha Book Two

June began, "I didn't know, but I dreamed that you were here, somewhere in this world, waiting for me, dreaming about me."

Gus responded, "I couldn't see your face in my mind, but I felt you in my heart, to the depth of me."

And they alternated saying, "I felt you inside of me, felt you in the rhythm of my breathing and the beating of my heart."

"I wasn't sure how to find you, or even where to look, but I had faith that we would meet and our eyes would know."

"And our hands would touch."

"And our hearts would melt."

And together, speaking as one voice, they said. "And our spirits would merge as one."

They continued, "I see you now. You stand firm and strong. You are graceful and beautiful and divine."

"You are radiant and your inner spirit speaks to mine."

Little Buddha Book Two

"They draw us together, in a sacred harmony."

And then together, they ended saying, "We offer our lives to each other in this world and beyond."

They held hands and Janine placed one of her hands over theirs. She asked for the rings to be presented. Jamie came over, holding Schrodinger in her arms. Claire stepped forward and untied the knot to release the rings and handed them to her mom.

Janine held them aloft where they glowed in the moonlight. She handed a ring to June and one to Gus and said, "I ask you to always remember that these rings represent the circle of love you have for each other and that we have for you. This is a wedding of all present. We are your family and will always be with you, always in your hearts and in your dreams. As you place rings on each other's finger, know that you are loved and that you love. See in each other the presence of the divine and be blessed."

With that, June and Gus placed rings on each other's fingers and kissed to the sounds of waves gently crashing on the shore.

Little Buddha Book Two

Everyone cheered and shouted and whistled. There was such a sense of joy in the air. I was profoundly impacted by the beauty and simplicity of the ceremony, their vows and the ring exchange. Perhaps someday I might have to chance to celebrate a marriage like this.

After the ceremony, we returned to Janine and Claire's cottage to enjoy a fabulous spread of many different foods and beverages. That's when another ceremony took place. Each of us had decided we wanted to hand the wedding couple a meaningful gift.

June and Gus sat together on the couch and we paraded by them, one at a time, handing them our gifts, which they opened. I gave them a copy of my favorite book, The Kin Of Ata Are Waiting by Dorothy Bryant. I love it so much that I read it every year.

Doug handed them a mantel clock. It had a revolving dial that showed a three masted ship on the high seas moving from night toward day.

Doug said to them, "Maybe sometimes when it chimes, you can think of me on my life's journey."

Little Buddha Book Two

Maheer walked over and handed them a beautiful gift bag. June reached in and pulled out an intricately detailed metal framed candle holder. There were words cut into the edge that read, 'may you always keep your inner light glowing'.

Janine reached over and handed Gus a large box. Once unwrapped, he and June could see that it was a display shelf.

Janine explained, "It's for all of the small keepsakes you find in your world travels."

Claire stood and came over to June and handed her one of the decorated hearts from the alleyway fence. She'd customized it by painting the date of their wedding and a sun and a moon. Claire told Gus and June that everyone who had attended their wedding had signed the back of the heart.

Jamie was the last to present the couple with a gift. Actually, she had two. The first was a photo album for them to record all of their trip highlights and the second was a framed photo of the wedding ceremony, complete with Schrodinger's footprints at the bottom. I guess the ring-bearer deserved some special attention.

Little Buddha Book Two

Gus and June were thrilled with all of their presents and said together, "We see you. We thank you for believing in our dreams and we love you all."

June turned to Claire, a wry smile on her face and said, "I can't ever thank you enough for your coded message to me. I am so incredibly grateful to you."

I looked over at Claire, remembering the letters inside the flowers on the envelopes she'd sent me. I remembered they were some special code, but I had no idea what they said.

I asked, "So June, can you share the message? What did it say?"

June looked at me, then at Gus and grinned.

It said, "Come visit me, I have someone for you to meet."

June leaned over and hugged Gus. What an incredible story that would be for them to tell as they traveled around the world.

Little Buddha Book Two

It was the next day and many of us were leaving. Maheer had already dropped June and Gus at the airport and had come back to pick up Doug for the long ride home.

I'd said my goodbyes to Jamie and Claire and even to Schrodinger. It was just Janine and me now.

"I know that you already know that I'm going to see your father and go on a vision quest of my own, but what I also want you to know is how much I'm going to miss you. You've come to mean so much to me. I feel you here, in my heart, and I want you to know…"

Janine placed a finger to my lips to gently silence me and said, "Everything we'll ever need to know about each other will be in our eyes. I trust looks over words."

She smiled at me and her eyes danced. There was an incredible light in them. And there was a radiant love pouring out toward me. She reached her arms around me and said, "and I trust touch above all," and she kissed me on my lips. Pure heaven!

Little Buddha Book Two

exercises for going deeper

Little Buddha Book Two

going deeper
(exercises)

I want to offer you an opportunity to go deeper into the stories, so the following sections provide a suggestion for focus, an opening prayer/meditation and some questions to consider. Hopefully this will be helpful for those who would like to spend some time in self-study or perhaps, for group study and discussion.

Little Buddha Book Two

homecoming
opportunity for going deeper:

Think of something in your life that creates pain and suffering for you. Consider how it might be possible to transform it through the power of love using ideas from the story.

Little Buddha Book Two

homecoming
opening prayer/meditation

Take this moment to close your eyes and sink into your awesome loving self. Know that each of us is divine and that none of us 'deserves' a life of suffering and pain. We realize that life can and sometimes does feel unfair. Some things in our lives can't be undone, but we can allow our hearts to open, and in this opening, love can enter freely. If we allow it, each of us has so much to receive. We benefit from knowing that life renews itself. We benefit when we let the love that surrounds us, come inside. When we let it connect with the inside love already present within us. Often, we judge by appearances. We see ourselves as separate. We see everyone else as separate, but the truth is that we are all a part of the one, inseparable. What happens to one of us, happens to us all. And we each possess within us the power of transformative love. We can give it and receive it. We can choose to shift our perceptions. We can choose our intentions and pour our love over any experience, shifting any thunder into a rainbow. Let it be so. AMEN.

Little Buddha Book Two

homecoming
(questions)

Do you ever miss seeing some obvious things because you're so focused on one thing?

Is there anyone you feel "at home" with? What is it about them that makes you feel this way?

Do you have any meaningful rituals for when you're reunited with folks you love after a separation? What do you think of Janine and Claire's reunion ceremony?

What do you think about Claire's note to Maheer? Could you feel her love for him?

Have you ever sat among a stand of trees and been silent? How did it make you feel? If you haven't, would you consider doing it for the experience?

Have you ever taken time to fully consider another person's words and spent time 'feeling them' before responding? Did that feel different from your normal response?

What do you think of Bright Sky's statement to Claire (Nexahe, Nexie)?

Little Buddha Book Two

Were you surprised to learn an aspen grove is one organism? Do you think there are other observations you've made, like Claire, where the truth is much deeper than what appears on the surface?

Do you believe others can see the hurts in your heart like Bright Sky could see in Claire's?

Do you believe we can transform our perceptions of pain and suffering through love, through our radiant intentions and constant choice?

Little Buddha Book Two

more room
opportunity for going deeper:

If you were sitting in the chair in 'the room' what memory would you choose to re-experience? Sit and imagine it in as much detail as possible and see what happens.

Little Buddha Book Two

more room
opening prayer/meditation

Sit comfortably, close your eyes and relax to some music in your mind. Shift your awareness to your breathing. Let it be slow and smooth and easy. Find your rhythm. Feel inside you that you are breathing for mother earth. That her energy rises up through your feet. You are connected and aware of the grounding energy that supports you. Rest here.

Now feel the divine energy entering through the top of your head and moving downward through your whole body. Let it flow and run through you and bring you peace. Rest here for a moment.

Now shift your attention to your heart, where the two energies become one. Let the energy grow. Feel your heartbeat and know you are part of the divine.

Imagine looking back over the course of your life and knowing that every experience contained seeds of growth for you, even the ones that were difficult or hurtful. Perhaps especially these. Imagine realizing that everyone has suffered and part of them

Little Buddha Book Two

remains unhealed and unprepared to show love to others. A part of everyone is a prisoner to their own thoughts and feelings. Imagine that you possess the key to your own thoughts and feelings of guilt, shame, anger and unworthiness. Imagine knowing there is a way out of this prison. As you realize this, you can offer yourself and others your forgiveness. You can exercise your free will and choose a path of true liberation. You can blaze a new trail, releasing all of your pain and suffering, because your true nature is love. It is the divine energy inside of your breath, inside of your heart. Rest here and release all that no longer serves you. AMEN.

Little Buddha Book Two

more room
questions

If you could sit in the chair in 'the room' would you? Would you even if you knew you might re-live a painful memory?

Are there people in your life who feel YOU are their 'sunshine'? How does that make you feel?

Are there events from your life you would not be able to call 'glorious'?

If you meditate, do you bring up energy from the earth and bring down energy from the sky, to meet in your heart? How does it feel?

Do you have any painful memories from childhood? Do you think that understanding why they happened would be helpful or beneficial for you?

Have you ever been berated? If so, do you believe you might be able to forgive the person (without condoning their actions) if you understood them and what drove their behavior and actions?

Little Buddha Book Two

Were you surprised to find out about Henry's experience? Can you see how this shaped his lifelong actions?

Were you surprised to find out about Henry's teacher's experience? Do you find it possible to show compassion to both Henry and his teacher? What might prevent you from feeling compassion toward them?

Do you think it would feel 'glorious' to be able to release all the negative emotions attached to your hurtful experiences?

Do you sometimes feel like a prisoner to your emotions, unable to release them and be free?

Does Claire's statement appear too simple when she tells Sam that the answer is 'choice'?

Do you believe you can use your free will to choose to forgive all who have hurt you and to forgive yourself for whatever part you've played and set yourself free?

Little Buddha Book Two

the nature of water
opportunity for going deeper:

Think of a time in your life where you felt significant fear and consider whether you can find a way to release the fear, like Gus did during the storm.

Little Buddha Book Two

the nature of water
opening prayer/meditation

Bring your awareness to your breath. Imagine that you can see it as it enters into you and moves throughout your whole body. Watch as it gently passes out through your nose or your mouth. Smile as the rhythm of your breathing continues through you. Such a beautiful, simple, joyful action. In this relaxing place, allow your mind to drift. Do you realize that you are in charge of your own world? You have the choice to establish your own meanings about everything you experience. You may 'borrow' others meanings or create ones of your own. How liberating to know that you can create as you choose. Your will is free. If you feel fear, you can resist, you can fall prey, you can ignore, you can make any choice you wish. What do you wish? Are you brave enough to sit with your fears? To stand in their presence? To allow them to speak to you and to know their depth, for without this, it is so hard to move through and beyond them?

Know that the divine is always with you. Always there for support, guidance and love. The divine, by whatever name you choose, is present and whole and fully with you, ready to dream new dreams with you. Ready to hear

Little Buddha Book Two

your deepest concerns and fill you with unending love. Ready to stand with you through any experience, through every experience. Sit and feel the truth of this and know that the divine is with you always.

Little Buddha Book Two

the nature of water
questions

Do you believe there is any significance to numbers? What's your decision based on?

Claire says that for her, the number three stands for thought, word and action, which is the force that creates everything in our lives. How do you feel about this?

Do you believe that your 'intentions' give creative energy to your thoughts, words and actions?

How do, 'conceive, believe and act' relate to 'thought, word and action'? Are they meaningful concepts to you?

Do you know anyone whose eyes seem to 'see deeper' than others, like Sam says about Claire and Janine?

Do you think it's possible to change someone's countenance (emotional state) with a hug? Do you know anyone who does this?

If someone were to say, 'I see you', upon greeting you, what might you think they meant? Try saying it sometime, in the way

Little Buddha Book Two

Sam describes it and see what reaction(s) you receive.

What do you think of Gus's shift in awareness from identifying with the boat, to identifying with the water? Can you see how that released his fear? Does the story have implications for you?

Gus said he stopped fighting the fear and just gave in, then experienced peace and balance, despite the storm continuing. Could you do something like this? If you could, how might it change your life?

Claire and Janine held Maheer as he cried and 'just sat with him'. Sam's inclination was to try to 'fix' what was wrong. How do you react when someone is hurting?

Maheer thanked Gus for his story because it helped him release what he needed to let go of. Are their things you would be wise to release?

Little Buddha Book Two

"i am..."
opportunity for going deeper:

As Sam has done, you may want to complete two different lists. The first list is to write down one hundred answers to the question, "i am a..." and the second list is to write down one hundred answers to the question, "i am..." and see what thoughts and feelings arise for you.

(Consider this: one hundred was chosen on purpose because it forces you to go deeper, so try to stick with it, if you can.)

Little Buddha Book Two

"i am..."
opening prayer/meditation

Do you ever wonder who you are? There is so much we see and do in this life. When we don't immediately see and feel that we know all, we are tempted to make assumptions. We make these about ourselves and those who surround us. We fill in all of the blanks, perhaps to make better sense of the world. To unveil some of the mystery.

Do you ever wonder why you are here? Where did you come from and where are you going? Do you have any memories not of this life, but from another? Might it be possible for you to believe you came from a place of pure love? That your truest nature is this pure love. And it was all you ever knew until you came here, to this earth, where you can create and experience anything. You can feel joy and heartache, pain and pleasure, despair and dreams. Can you see that every action is open to you and that each choice and decision you make proclaims who you are here in this life.

Do you wonder what lies beyond this earth existence? Do you seek the truth and desire to remember?

Little Buddha Book Two

Consider that the truth is, you return to where you came from. To the pure ocean of bliss, where you are filled and overflowing with love. This is your true home. Rest in this knowing.

AMEN

Little Buddha Book Two

"i am…"
questions

How often do you make assumptions and 'fill in the blanks' about what others are thinking or doing? Do you find this way of reacting serves you?

What do you think you'd learn about yourself if you wrote down your own 100 answers to the question, "I am a…"?

Sam is constantly surprised by Claire and her ability to know things before they happen. Do you believe it's possible to know things in advance? If you know someone like this, do you enjoy the mystery of it?

What insights do you think you'd find by completing the second 100 answers to the question, "I am…"? How do you think it would differ from the first list?

Do you sometimes wonder, 'what you bring to the table' and what your contribution is to your relationships with others? What do you usually conclude? Do you recognize how valuable you are?

Little Buddha Book Two

If you completed the second list ("I am…"), what do you think the general nature of the answers would be?

How do you feel about the idea of 'labeling' events and experiences? Do you feel that by 'labeling' an experience, you make it difficult to receive any messages it has for you?

Do you believe your answers to the two assignments would change from year to year? If you'd done this five or ten years ago, would it be different today? If so, in what ways?

How do you feel and what do you think about Claire's description of the 'before life'? Do you feel there is any truth to it?

Do you believe that you can create and experience anything you choose here on earth? That your choices are limitless? Does this idea conflict with what you've been taught? Do you feel free to choose for yourself what to believe?

Are there any people in your life who you immediately feel a sense of 'kinship' with? If so, what does this mean to you?

Little Buddha Book Two

What do you think Sam meant when he asked Claire about 'remembering the truth' of who he is?

Do you feel there is a space inside of you that wants to be filled? If you do, how have you tried to fill it?

Do you agree with Claire's answer that 'love' is how we 'remember', that by feeling love inside you and choosing to share this love with others, that you 'remember the truth'?

Little Buddha Book Two

string theory
opportunity for going deeper:

Using Claire's description and explanation, consider setting up your own 'Celebration Journal' and choose one event from your life and spend time journaling an entry about the insights you find within the event.

Little Buddha Book Two

string theory
opening prayer/meditation

Is there space inside of you for new ideas? Is it possible for you to make shifts, to alter your awareness, to move beyond your present thoughts and feelings? The truth is, we can if that is what we choose. Imagine your whole life is made up of threads and each thread is a thought or feeling. And all of the threads are connected and interwoven. But the pattern that has been created doesn't seem entirely right to you. It doesn't fit. It feels too tight or too loose, and yet you are afraid to alter the design. Afraid that if you pull on one of the threads, it will all unravel. You've seen this happen to others and you've seen it in your own life. There may be great hesitation inside of you about this. But you also realize that keeping the pattern just as it is will mean feeling as you do right now for the rest of your life. And this idea may inspire you to want to change. You believe you would benefit from taking action. You realize it would be helpful to pull the loose threads. Something, something deep inside you tells you to pull the loose threads. And so, you do.

Know this, that by pulling the threads and feeling your true feelings about what each

Little Buddha Book Two

thread means to you, you can release whatever power they have over you. And amazingly, the threads can weave themselves into a new design and your fabric can become even stronger. Each time you pull on a loose thread and feel its message and shift your thoughts, your quilt becomes even more beautiful. Rest here and feel the wonder of this.

AMEN

Little Buddha Book Two

string theory
questions

Do you ever feel like Schrodinger, that you are so focused on one thing you don't seem to notice anything else? Would it help to recognize this and broaden your awareness?

What do you think about Claire's statements about each essence having a 'nature'? How often do you feel you evaluate others based on comparisons?

Do you ever feel 'bad' about yourself for pursuing one of your goals, regardless of the outcome? If so, what different choice could you make? Can you let yourself off the hook of self-judgment and shift your awareness?

Have you ever met someone with a very strong 'vibration'? What do you believe accounts for this?

How would it feel to be referred to as someone's 'very own ray of sunshine', as Claire does to Jamie, about Sam?

How do you feel about Jamie's trying to shift people's opinions about her from being 'blind' to being 'funny'?

Little Buddha Book Two

Do you find that you experience 'object lessons' in your life? What was the last one you remember and what insights did you experience?

What are your thoughts and feelings about Janine's 'Celebration Journal'? Can you believe that all events in your life work toward your benefit? If not, what obstacles stand in your way?

What do you think about Janine's belief that no matter how an event in her life 'appears', that if it appears 'negative', there is an equal or greater 'positive' outcome to it?

In the middle of explaining her example. Claire notices that Sam is upset and asks him to close his eyes and breathe, so he can relax. Do you have a way of relaxing when you start to get upset? Is there a practice that would benefit you so that you could release stresses that you experience before they 'get out of control'?

What do you think about what Janine taught Claire, that if you don't 'feel your feelings' they can become 'loose threads' and there is no telling when they might unravel?

Little Buddha Book Two

How do you feel about Sam's "Feelings Journal"? Is it a practice you believe might be valuable for you?

Do you believe it would be meaningful for you to try to find the message(s) inside of each of your life experiences, especially the 'big events'?

What do you think about Claire's statement that her disease wasn't happening TO her, rather it was happening THROUGH her?

Do you have any energy practices where you align with the universe's energy and let it move through you? How does it feel to you? Have you ever used it to help yourself heal?

Little Buddha Book Two

sparks
opportunity for going deeper:

Imagine going on a vision quest where you have no time constraints and are by yourself in a beautiful setting. What do you think would happen as you move inward into the depth of you?

Little Buddha Book Two

sparks
opening prayer/meditation

Close your eyes and breathe into a quiet space. With each breath, imagine releasing all control. Ask spirit guides to come and be with you, even if you've never done this before, even if there is some doubt in you. Let go and ask them to come and be with you. Allow your mind to be free and let it drift. Open your heart. Ask it to be a welcoming place where love and strength can enter and grow. Breathe freely in and out and watch as peace surrounds you, bathing you in warmth and softness. Ask your spirit guides to share their messages of love, support and guidance with you. Let their clear words and unconditional love settle over you. Open yourself even further, releasing all the points of control you normally hold so dear. Let them fall away. Allow spirit all the way in. And as spirit moves and fills you with love, notice it is no longer important or necessary to judge by appearances, because now you know this was done only as a means of self-protection. The truth is everything serves your greatest good. With spirits help you can stay present and see beyond first appearances. You can look past all labels and any previous need you had to remain separate. You are a part of the whole and everything is a part of you. No matter how

Little Buddha Book Two

events arrive in your life, they are each a part of the pattern, each here to serve your greatest good. Even if they feel 'negative' to you, uncomfortable, difficult or objectionable, they each possess equal or greater value than how they first appeared to you. Ask spirit to be with the deepest part of you, so that the truth of this becomes clear. Allow spirit to show you that each experience holds inside of it a 'spark'. A 'spark' which can ignite an awareness of the truth. The truth that we can create and experience this life any way we choose. Open to the idea that every experience and every fear you have point the way to the truth. They are sparks that flare up, creating light to help you 'remember'. To know the truth that there is only love. To help you shift your awareness so that in all things you first see love, feel love and give love. That it overflows from you. This is the truth.

AMEN

Little Buddha Book Two

sparks
questions

Do you find that labeling' an experience makes it challenging to remain open to any messages it might have for you? Next time you find yourself using a 'label', see if you can wait to see what the messages are.

Can you imagine drawing a heart on your bathroom window with the word, 'me' in the middle of it? Would you say that you 'love yourself'?

Do you 'know things in your knower', that place where you feel the truth without question?

Have you ever felt the 'vibration of the universe that Janine and Sam experienced? Would you like to experience it or experience it more often? How do you think this would feel to do this daily?

Sam believes that a part of Janine's beauty is because she loves herself. What do you think about this? Do you believe it's true for everyone?

Little Buddha Book Two

Do you believe you have spiritual guides? Do you feel that LIA (love in action) is available to you? Are you interested in asking for her help with your life? Do you think she loves you?

What do you think of Janine's statement that Lia wants what you want or something even better?

Do you believe that Lia (one of Janine's names for god)/(or whatever name you use for god) is interactive in your life? Does god help you? Can you trust god?

When you ask or pray for something specific to happen in your life, do you judge whether you are answered based on immediate appearances? Are you open to waiting and watching what happens and remaining 'present' for any and all messages that occur?

What do you think about Janine's 'celebration journal'? How do you think this would work in your life?

Janine tells Sam that every experience in her life has become meaningful and connected and exists to serve her greatest good. What do you think about this way of living?

Little Buddha Book Two

Do you think it's possible to find meaning and value in every one of your experiences, especially the most challenging?

Do you 'pounce on sun spots', thinking that what you believe to be the truth turns out not to be?

What do you think about Janine's statement that "the essence of every experience is a 'spark', which can ignite an awareness of the truth'?"

What are your thoughts and feeling about Janine saying that our life on earth is a 'grand illusion', designed for you to experience anything you wish, yet it is not the real truth?

Do you see how each of your fears serves as a 'spark', because each flares up and creates 'light' to see the truth?

What do you feel and think about Janine's statement that "every fear unerringly points the way to love"?

Do you believe you could sit with your fears, like Janine did? What help would you need in order to be able to do this?

Little Buddha Book Two

How do you feel about the idea of 'awakening' that Janine talks about?

Little Buddha Book Two

seeds
opportunity for going deeper:

Sam's 'calendar project' is pretty expansive and intriguing. Try a scaled down version for yourself by choosing either his categories or categories of your own. Then pick a workable number, maybe starting with twelve, representing one entry for each month of the year. Then write down your thoughts and answers to the categories, as a celebration of your life. If you're enjoying it, add more as time goes by.

Little Buddha Book Two

seeds
opening prayer/meditation

Relax your eyes by looking into the distance. Let them softly go unfocused and close. Ask your breathing to change shape, to lengthen and deepen. Feel your heart beat evenly and know that it pumps blood to every part of your body to keep you healthy. Know that love flows through you and radiates from you to support you and the whole world.

In this sweet place, see in your mind's eye one of your favorite places in the world. Imagine every detail, the scents surrounding you and the feeling sensations to your touch. Imagine the wonderful sights and the tastes you associate with it. What sounds do you hear? Let them all sink in and be with you. Allow each of your senses to increase, to blossom, to magnify. Sit with this joy.

Imagine the clouds are swirling gently in the sky, forming an almost perfect white canopy above you, complete except for one small opening. Look up and notice through this window in the clouds, there is an host of brilliant sun rays. They are streaking to the ground and surrounding you, dazzling you. You are completely transfixed by their beauty.

Little Buddha Book Two

You feel so incredibly alive. Each of your senses is sharp. And you hear a voice, a smooth golden voice. A voice you know is speaking directly to you. It is a voice of love. You feel this to the very core of you. There is something so familiar to you about this voice and you are drawn to it. And there are words. They drift down to you amidst the radiant streaming rays. You feel yourself suspended, waiting, collecting each word until the voice falls into silence.

The words, the precious words. Words you will keep in your heart forever. You repeat them over and over to yourself…"my beloved, oh my beloved, fear nothing and love everything, as I love you." Feel the warmth of these words. Fill your heart with them. Know they belong to you. They are yours forever. Keep them near you as you wake and walk out into the world.

AMEN

Little Buddha Book Two

seeds
questions

How would it feel to you to have someone ask you, "how has your journey been since I saw you last?"

What do you think about Sam's 'calendar project'? Does the idea appeal to you?

Do you use 'affirmation statements' in your life? Are they helpful? Do you believe them?

How do you feel about Sam's calendar project as a way to celebrate your life? Would you say you have a lot of memories worth celebrating?

What part does 'gratitude' play in your life? Are you most grateful for the small, medium or large things in your life?

If you reviewed your life, do you believe you'd find that your 'spiritual journey' is a series of dots?

Is there a lot of 'good stuff' in your life? If you were to sit and think about them, how many could you come up with?

Little Buddha Book Two

Are there 'special people' in your life you'd like to celebrate? How would you like to celebrate them?

Do you think it would be fun to relive and celebrate the experiences of your life, looking over your entries and some collected photos and memorabilia? If not, what would prevent it from being fun?

Have you ever had an experience like what happened to Sam on the beach, where he felt wholly and intimately loved by god? If so, how has that changed your life?

What are your thoughts about the 'seed experiment'? Did you think it would turn out the way it did?

What do you think about Sam's initial explanation and about the metaphor?

How do you feel about Janine, Claire and Jamie's explanations about the seed metaphor?

What do you think about Sam's answer/explanation of the seed metaphor?

Little Buddha Book Two

change orders
opportunity for going deeper:

Sit quietly and ponder for a moment the meaning of the story. Then, take a piece of paper and write down all of the dreams you have for your life. Write them ALL down and then, using whatever materials you like, create a visual representation of your dreams. Consider writing on a strip of cloth, like in the story and hanging up somewhere you'll see it often. Or write on post-it notes and put them up around the house or at work, places you'll notice. Use your imagination and make it fun.

Little Buddha Book Two

change orders
opening prayer/meditation

Imagine there is a switch sitting in front of you. At this moment it is "off" because you feel somehow disconnected. You feel there is some distance between what you see and feel and what you dream is possible. Somehow you don't feel powerful enough or hopeful enough to bring your dreams to life. All of this can change.

Look at the switch carefully. See the contours of it. See your hand reaching for it and feel your fingers come to rest upon it. There is a certain knowing forming inside of you. A recognition that something very important is about to happen. Give your fingers permission to move the switch to the "on" position. See it happen now and sense the excitement.

You are now connected. Connected to the source of all power. A power that reaches in and through you. Reaches to your very essence. You know with absolute certainty that you are connected to the power of love. You know that you can do anything, change anything, change everything. There is an enormous sense of gratitude streaming through you. It raises you up higher and

Little Buddha Book Two

higher. So high you take flight. Flight into the dream world. You revel in the magnificence of this place where all that appears is truly real. Everything here is ready to be made manifest. Ready to become a part of you through the power of love. Soar with your dreams. Gather them to you and place them in your heart. Bring them all with you, as you drift back to your earth life. As you come home, let each of your dreams inspire your actions. Feel their love inspired power flow through your grateful heart. Remember them often.

AMEN

Little Buddha Book Two

change orders
questions

Have you ever volunteered at a community gathering place or shelter? What was it like for you? Did you feel love present?

Do you often "dream while you are awake"?

If you sat quietly and opened yourself, what dreams do you think would flow into your awareness? Take a minute to see, then write them down.

Do you believe there are limits to your dreams? If so, what are the obstacles that you see? Is there a way for you to shift your beliefs and move beyond the obstacles?

What does it take to make dreams come into your life?

Have you ever kept a 'gratitude journal'? If you started one today, what would you record in it?

What do you think about Janine's statement, that "gratitude" inspires your dreams, gives them energy to become real, exceeds all limits, opens your heart wide, restores your balance and lifts you up?

Little Buddha Book Two

How do you think it might change your life if you wrote down three things you were grateful for each morning or each evening?

Do you trust your heart and spirit to speak to you and help you create your most meaningful life here? If not, what challenges come up for you?

What do you think about Janine's statement that, "each person can change anything in their life and that all changes come from your sense of love and gratitude"?

Little Buddha Book Two

sign language
opportunity for going deeper

Think about a person you find somewhat challenging to deal with and imagine seeing them as a divine being, created and existing as pure love. Try to see beyond their surface appearance and imagine how you might interact with them the next time you see them.

Little Buddha Book Two

sign language
opening prayer/meditation

Do you know who you are? Perhaps you get stuck in our grand illusion, which makes it hard to see yourself clearly. Perhaps you keep track of all of the events of your life, many of which you criticize yourself for, so that you experience many difficulties and your true self remains hidden from you. It is so easy to see the surface of our lives. To score every perceived failure. To lament every unattained goal. To regret every harsh word and gesture done by us, done to us. Perhaps your anger holds you tightly in its grasp or you feel closed off from the world, drawn inward, needing to protect yourself. Perhaps you are afraid to open to love, to be loved. Perhaps the surface of your life is too real for you and that you find it hard to imagine knowing you are more than this. So much more than this.

Would you like to see with new eyes? With a new heart, one which sees the truth? The truth of who you really are?

Close your eyes for a moment. Imagine your eyes being washed, cleansed, refreshed, ready for a new vision. Open your eyes and open your heart. Imagine you are facing a

Little Buddha Book Two

mirror. Allow your gaze to fall upon your reflection. Look deeply into your own eyes. Know that there is a depth to them that is infinite. That is connected to the one source of all power and love. To the divine center of all creation. This is who you are…the eyes of love, able to see into every darkness and bring light to it. Able to renew and refresh, to start again. And this time, to start with the awareness that you are made fully of love. A radiance and brilliance beyond your present imagining. You are connected to the source of all love. Connected in such a way that you will always feel it. This is who you are, love incarnate in the world. You are part of the divine, living and moving in this beautiful world. In all things, you can choose the path of love. You are love.

AMEN

Little Buddha Book Two

sign language
questions

Do you know 'sign language'? If so, do you notice how those with hearing impairments respond to you, while signing?

Do you look into the eyes of the person you are 'speaking' with? What do you see? How does that compare with what they are 'saying/signing' to you?

Claire tells Sam, "there is no 'them', there is only 'us'." What do you think about that statement? If we could always see and treat everyone as part of 'us', how would that change things?

Do you think you make assumptions based on appearances? Does this seem like another example of 'labeling'? If you looked deeper, would it benefit you and the person you're observing?

In the story Claire tells Sam that Graham projects all of his fears into the world because they are too intense for him to hold inside. Do you know anyone who does this? Would it be possible for you to 'look past their appearance' and see the person as whole and lovable?

Little Buddha Book Two

What do you think of what Claire tells Sam, about being able to see beyond Graham's anger and about reading his 'signs' that he is open to her? Is this something you can do?

When you encounter someone who is challenging to communicate with, do you think it is possible they are reading your 'hesitant' signs and reacting to them? To improve communication, what might you be able to do?

Do you think it's possible that when a person reacts negatively toward you, they are afraid of you pushing them away first? Do you think this could be one of their emotional survival techniques?

What do you think about the concept of spiritual DNA, a blueprint for your spiritual experiences here on earth? How do you feel about the concept of 'free will', which gives you the ability to make choices AND that nothing about your blueprint is set in stone?

What do you think of Claire's statement that, "inside your spiritual DNA, there is an inherent ability to heal any condition or disease you experience?"

Little Buddha Book Two

Claire tells Sam that, "the healing process is all about moving from fear to love. It's important to know what each fears message is for us. It's important that we ask ourselves, what am I to know that this experience is here to show me. And then it becomes important to listen and then move into faith, because what you believe is what you experience." What are your thoughts about this?

How did it strike you when you read Claire's statement, "Sam, I'm not saying that disease doesn't 'appear' real to us, nor that we don't experience it as if it is real. But I am saying it isn't the whole truth. It is the expression of our fears. And these fears generate tangible physical, emotional, mental and spiritual outcomes."?

Do you feel like Sam, that if you tried Claire's process of healing and weren't successful, then you've set yourself up to feel even more the victim?

Do you believe someone could heal from a condition or disease using Claire and Michael's process of sitting with their fears, listening to them, giving them love, discovering their message(s) and then releasing the fears and then filling their space with love?

Little Buddha Book Two

new beginnings
opportunity for going deeper:

If you spent some time reviewing your life, would certain people come to mind that you feel very grateful for? Consider choosing one of them and send them your love. You could do this any way you feel comfortable; a card, a letter, a phone call or holding them in your heart with love. How do you think it would feel to do this?

Little Buddha Book Two

new beginnings
opening prayer/meditation

Is there someone from your life that you truly loved, who is no longer physically present on this earth? Maybe there is more than one, perhaps there are many. Spend a moment and bring them into your mind and into your heart. See each of them clearly. What is it about them that you hold so dear? What did you share? What did you create? Was there a turning point when you gave away your heart to them? When you knew you loved them? When you saw your love blossom and grow and find a place within you?

Imagine how much richer your life is because of them.

Perhaps remembering them touches you with some sorrow. A kind of sorrow that reaches deep inside of you because you cannot touch them, feel their arms around you, feel their kiss upon you. There are many kinds of grief, all of them challenging in their own ways. Can you sit with this? Sit with the grief, letting it rest inside of you? Would you like to release this grief? You can. You always can. Would you like to free it from you, so that all that remains is your beautiful love for them?

Little Buddha Book Two

Take a moment and imagine filling a balloon with each pain you feel. Put them all inside the balloon and let it go. Release it skyward. Watch it take flight and move higher and higher, till it almost fades out of sight. Imagine, in its final moment before disappearing, seeing it burst in all directions. There is color and light, beautiful beyond anything you've ever seen before. And you know that this radiant shower of brilliance represents the truth of love. The love that exists now and forever for all who have touched you and become a part of you, a part of your life. They are within you, inseparable and ever present. How divine.

AMEN

Little Buddha Book Two

new beginnings
questions

Would you like to go on a 'vision quest' of your own? If so, are there any obstacles that might stand in your way? Can they be surmounted?

Claire still feels spiritually connected to her father John, who is deceased. Are there people close to you who are deceased, but whose presence you still feel in your life?

Do you sometimes find it hard to accept mercy, forgiveness and love from others because you haven't forgiven yourself for something?

Do you feel a connection to a 'spiritual father' or 'spiritual mother', like what Claire describes? If so, how does it make you feel?

Do you have some deep personal spiritual experience(s) you don't ordinary share? What would inspire you to share it/them with others?

Is there anyone in your life that you are as grateful for as Gus is to the people of Greenland? What makes you so appreciative?

Little Buddha Book Two

What do you think of June and Gus's wedding vows and the simplicity of the ceremony?

How do you feel about Janine's wedding pronouncement, especially where she includes everyone as a part of June and Gus's wedding?

How did you feel during the 'giving of the wedding gifts'?

What do you think Sam will experience during his 'vision quest'?

Little Buddha Book Two

Little Buddha Book Two Notes

Little Buddha Book Two

Made in the USA
Lexington, KY
22 July 2018